NVivo for Mac Essentials

Welcoming Mac-users to the NVivo world

By Bengt M. Edhlund & Allan G. McDougall

FORM & KUNSKAP AB
INFORMATIONTECHNOLOGY

FORM & KUNSKAP AB • P.O.BOX 4 • SE-645 06 STALLARHOLMEN • SWEDEN • +46 152 201 80
SALES@FORMKUNSKAP.COM • WWW.FORMKUNSKAP.COM

NVIVO
NVivo is a registered trademark of QSR International Pte Ltd.

MAC
Mac and Macintosh are registered trademarks of Apple Inc.

WORD, EXCEL, ONENOTE
Word, Excel, and OneNote are registered trademarks of Microsoft Corporation.

ENDNOTE
EndNote is a registered trademark of Thomson Reuters.

EVERNOTE
Evernote is a registered trademark of Evernote Corporation.

LIMITED LIABILITY
This document describes the functions and features valid for NVivo for Mac. Form & Kunskap is unable to predict or anticipate changes in service performance or functionality of later versions or changes of respective software that might influence or change the described features.

COPYRIGHT FORM & KUNSKAP AB 2016
The content of this document is subject to regulation according to the Swedish law on copyright, 1960:729. The said contents must not be reproduced or distributed in any form without a written consent from Form & Kunskap Stockholm Aktiebolag. The restrictions are valid for the entire document or parts thereof and include electronic storage, display on VDU or a similar device and audio or video recording.

ISBN 978-1-365-18746-9

FOREWARD

Welcome to **NVivo for Mac Essentials**, a comprehensive guide to the world's most popular qualitative data analysis software. This book has two authors with distinct lenses on NVivo. Bengt Edhlund is an engineer and trainer with decades of experience teaching and writing about research software. Dr. Allan McDougall is a qualitative researcher who has used NVivo on projects using discourse analysis, ethnography, thematic coding, and surveys.

Building on our other books that explore NVivo, PubMed, EndNote and a variety of other tools and utilities, NVivo for Mac contains something for users of all skill and experience levels. Not only do we break down the functional components of NVivo in all their intricacy, we also strive to provide practical, anecdotal advice for using NVivo for Mac. Whether you are just getting started or you are writing up, we are confident this book contains valuable advice that will streamline every stage of your work.

Form & Kunskap AB, founded by Bengt in 1993, is a training company focused on software solutions for academic researchers. Our philosophy is that a single software will never be the only solution for researchers and research teams. In many ways, research is like woodworking: a quality product will always be the result of combining many tools and techniques. Also like woodworking, there are always several ways to achieve the final goal. We teach researchers how to take advantage of the strengths of industry leading software and how to work around the drawbacks. This book provides the essential foundation for you to success with NVivo for Mac. Our years of experience have taught us one central lesson that we impart through this book: the better you understand what can be done and how, the more efficiently and effectively you will finish your work.

Please enjoy our book and feel free to contact us at any time at: info@formkunskap.com

TABLE OF CONTENTS

1. INTRODUCING NVIVO FOR MAC 9
   - Welcome to NVivo for Mac Essentials 9
   - What is NVivo for Mac? 10
   - A Crucial Note on NVivo Projects 12
   - Visualizing your Project 12
   - Exploring this Book 13
   - Graphic Conventions 14
   - Before you Install NVivo for Mac 15
   - Handling Other File Formats 15
2. THE NVIVO INTERFACE 17
   - The Navigation View & Folders 20
   - The List View 22
   - The Detail View 25
   - Copying, Cutting, and Pasting 26
   - Ribbon Tabs 29
   - Application Preferences 31
   - Alternate Screen Layouts 36
3. BEGINNING YOUR PROJECT 37
   - Creating a New Project 37
   - Sources & Project Size 38
   - Project Properties 39
   - Merging Projects 43
   - Exporting Project Data 43
   - Saving Projects 44
   - Compact a Project 44
   - Closing NVivo 44
4. HANDLING TEXT SOURCES 45
   - Importing Documents 45
   - Exporting a Document 48
   - External Items 49
   - Exporting an External Item 51
5. EDITING TEXT IN NVIVO 53
   - Formatting Text 53
   - Aligning Paragraphs 54
   - Finding and Navigating Text 54
   - Selecting Text 55
   - Inserting Images and Dates 55
   - Zooming 55
   - About Printing from NVivo 55
   - Limitations in Editing Documents in NVivo 56
6. HANDLING PDF SOURCES 59
   - Importing PDF Files 59

	Opening a PDF Item	62
	Exporting a PDF Item	62
7.	HANDLING AUDIO- AND VIDEO-SOURCES	65
	Importing Media Files	66
	Creating a New Media Item	68
	Opening a Media Item	70
	Playing Media Items	71
	Linking from a Media Item	76
	Exporting a Media Item	76
8.	HANDLING PICTURE SOURCES	77
	Importing Picture Files	77
	Opening a Picture Item	80
	Selecting a Region and Creating a Picture Log	81
	Editing Pictures	82
	Linking from a Picture Item	82
	Exporting a Picture Item	82
9.	MEMOS, LINKS, AND ANNOTATIONS	83
	Memos	83
	Exploring Links in the List View	83
	Exporting a Memo	90
	Annotations	91
	Hyperlinks	93
10.	INTRODUCING NODES	95
	Theme Nodes and Case Nodes	95
	Creating a Node	97
	Building Hierarchical Nodes	99
	Merging Nodes	100
	Exporting a Node	101
	The Folder Structure for Nodes	102
11.	CLASSIFICATIONS	103
	Case Classifications	104
	Source Classifications	104
	Creating a Case Classification	104
	Creating a Source Classification	105
	Customizing a Classification	106
	Working with the Classification Sheet	109
	Importing a Classification Sheet	111
	Exporting Classification Sheets	115
12.	CODING	117
	The Coding Panel	117
	Drag-and-Drop Coding	119
	Menus and Right-Click	119
	In Vivo Coding	121
	Coding by Queries	121
	Visualizing your Coding	122

    Coding a PDF-Item 125
    Coding a Media Item 127
    Coding a Picture Item 128
13. QUERIES 131
    Word Frequency Queries 132
    Text Search Queries 134
    Coding Queries 140
    Matrix Coding Queries 142
14. COMMON QUERY FEATURES 145
    Saving a Query 145
    Spread Coding 145
    Saving a Result 145
    About the Results Folder 145
    Editing a Query 146
    Last Run Query Option 146
15. HANDLING BIBLIOGRAPHIC DATA 147
    Importing Bibliographic Data 149
    The PDF Source Item 151
    The Linked Memo 153
    The External Source Item 154
    A New Source Classification 156
16. ABOUT QUESTIONNAIRES AND DATASETS 157
    Importing Datasets 157
    Opening a Dataset 162
    Exporting Datasets 162
    Coding Datasets 162
    Autocoding Datasets 162
17. INTERNET AND SOCIAL MEDIA 169
    Introducing NCapture 169
    Exporting websites with NCapture 169
    Importing Websites with NCapture 171
    Social Media Data and NCapture 173
    Capturing Social Media Data with NCapture 175
    Importing Social Media Data from NCapture 176
    Analyzing Social Media Datasets 178
    Autocoding a Dataset from Social Media 178
    Installing NCapture 178
    Check your Version of NCapture 178
18. USING ONENOTE WITH NVIVO 179
19. COLLABORATING WITH NVIVO 183
    Current User 183
    Coding Comparison Query 185
    Tips for Teamwork 187
    A Note on Cloud-computing 188
    A Note on NVivo Server 188

20. VISUALIZATIONS	189
Mind Maps	189
Hierarchy Charts	193
Explore Diagrams	197
Comparison Diagrams	199
21. HELP FUNCTIONS IN NVIVO	201
Help Documents Online	201
Search	201
NVivo Help	202
Keyboard Shortcuts	202
Getting Started Guide	202
Release Notes	202
Tutorials	202
FAQs	202
Support and Technical Issues	202
Screen Shots	203
Software Versions and Service Packs	204
22. GLOSSARY	205
INDEX	213

1. INTRODUCING NVIVO FOR MAC
Welcome to NVivo for Mac Essentials

Welcome to NVivo for Mac Essentials, your guide to the world's most powerful Mac-based qualitative data analysis software. The purpose of this book is to provide a comprehensive, usable, practical guide to using NVivo for Mac to streamline your qualitative and mixed-methods research. There is no one right way to use NVivo, but we the authors have enough collective experience to offer some best practices that will save you time and ensure you understand NVivo's best features.

For beginners, you will find explanations of key concepts and recommendations for starting your first NVivo project, importing your data, analyzing your data, and sharing your findings with collaborators. Some people find it hard to wrap their heads around NVivo, and you might be one of those people. Perhaps you have been playing around with the software already and you don't really 'get it'. This book offers that one simple description of what to do with NVivo and how you can make it work for you.

For advanced users, you will find useful instructions on how to use advanced NVivo features like handling bibliographic data, importing data from social media, and using visualizations to communicate with friends and collegues. We also provide advanced commentaries on a number of applications for NVivo features we have found successful over the years.

Bengt M. Edhlund, MScEE
Bengt Edhlund is the author of several books, including *NVivo 11 Essentials* (Windows). He is Scandinavia's leading research software trainer. As a former telecommunications engineer, Bengt has published 22 books on academic informatics tools such as NVivo, EndNote, PubMed, and Excel. All of Bengt's books are available in English and Swedish. He has trained researchers from every corner of the globe, including Canada, Sweden, Norway, China, Egypt, Uganda, and Vietnam. A trainer who takes pride in his students' success, Bengt provides all of his clients with customized NVivo support solutions via Skype or email.

Allan G. McDougall, PhD
A former student of Bengt's, Allan is a qualitative researcher with extensive NVivo experience. He has used NVivo in a collaborative academic environment on a number of diverse projects related to his area of qualitative health research. While Bengt knows every facet of NVivo's various functions, Allan is an NVivo user who provides

practical tips from his personal experiences applying NVivo to create dozens of qualitative research solutions.

What is NVivo for Mac?

Whoever you are and whatever you do, if you collect data you will at some point need to bring order and structure to that data. For qualitative researchers, this can include work using grounded theory, phenomenology, ethnography, discourse analysis, surveys, organizational studies or mixed-methods approaches.

NVivo for Mac allows researchers to organize and analyze a wide variety of data, including but not limited to, documents, images, audio, video, questionnaires and web / social media content. We have worked with researchers tasked with analyzing hundreds of interviews and focus group discussions, and researchers tasked with analyzing thousands of surveys blending quantitative and written data. Although at one time researchers were able to analyze data using paper-based systems, NVivo allows for the fast and easy analysis of large datasets for both individuals and multi-user teams.

NVivo was introduced as a Windows application in 2006. NVivo for Mac- was first launched 2014. When released, NVivo for Mac was missing the vast majority of product features found in its PC contemporary, NVivo 10. Frankly, NVivo for Mac was a disappointment to experienced NVivo users. Although we were seasoned PC users, we both purchased Mac computers in order to beta test the software. And although we were positioned to write this book 2 years ago, we simply felt that the software was not useful enough for us to begin recommending to colleagues nor to begin using in training.

However, over the past 2 years, QSR International has greatly improved the product. Although it still lacks numerous features when compared to the PC version of the software (NVivo 11 at the time of this writing), it contains the majority of what we might call the 'foundational' features. The current features and comparisons between product editions and features are listed here as they become available:

http://www.qsrinternational.com/product/product-feature-comparison

Key Components of an NVivo Project

The purpose of this section is familiarizing you with some of the NVivo terminology you will need to understand. **Sources**, **Nodes**, **Coding,** and **Queries** are the building blocks of an NVivo project. This book provides in-depth explanations of these concepts and you can explore each one by reading each chapter in order, or using the glossary to pick and choose topics of interest.

Below is a simplified diagram of an NVivo project's key components:

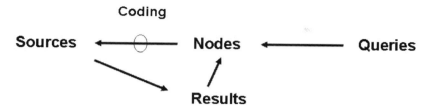

Sources are data. Sources can be documents, audio, video and image files, memos, websites, research articles, social media data, surveys, or entire websites. Sources can be imported into NVivo or they can be linked from other locations like the web. Some Sources, like text documents, can also be created directly inside NVivo using its built in word processor.

Nodes are 'virtual' containers for your data. They can contain everything from an entire file from you're your dataset, like an audio file, to small segment of data, like a sentence of text. Importantly, nodes do not literally contain your data; they refer to your data so in this sense they are virtual. A node is a like a hyperlink to a section of your dataset, and like hyperlinks the data does not disappear when you delete the link.

We will discuss Nodes in more detail later, but it is also important to recognize that nodes can also be concepts or organizational structures based on your own ideas. Nodes can designate properties, phenomena, or keywords that characterize aspects of your data.Nodes also allow you to add information about your data like the demographic information on research participants—this type of information is often called metadata. Later in the book, we will explain the important distinction between two types of Nodes: **Theme Nodes** and **Case Nodes**—suffice it to say for now that Case Nodes use metadata to organize the practical components of your research and Theme Nodes use conceptual information to relay analytic findings.

You have probably already heard the term **Coding**, but if not you should know that it is one of the most important concepts in qualitative research. Coding means grouping assortments oftext segments, audio snippets, video segments, or survey comments. Put simply, Coding is the activity of building Nodes. Later, we'll discuss how you can use NVivo's variety of coding tools to organize large portions of your dataset.

Queries underpin how qualitative data analysis generates research results. Whereas coding creates an organizational structure across a dataset, Queries find connections across that structure. They are special searches and filters that can be saved and reused as your project develops. Results of queries can also be saved, used to generate Nodes, data matrices, and data visualizations like charts and word clouds.

A Crucial Note on NVivo Projects

When working with NVivo, it is important to understand that the word project has two meanings. The first, more conventional meaning is simply your research project. But in this book we will use another meaning for the term: when we say **Project**, we mean the primary NVivo **Project file**. As we discuss later, NVivo creates a single file that will serve as an amalgamation of all Project Items, which includes Sources, Coding, Queries, and a host of other analytic units like **Diagrams** and **Sets**. NVivo allows you to organize your data into both **Project Items** and then to arrange them into folders.

Importantly, like Nodes, items and folders in NVivo are 'virtual' in relation to a Windows-based or Mac-based environment. In an NVivo Project, folders are similar to Windows or Mac OSX folders, but NVivo has special rules for how folders are handled—for example only certain types of folders are allowed to be organized hierarchically, and certain types of folders can only accommodate certain types of items. Like Finder in the Mac OSX operating system, Project Items and folders can be edited, copied, cut, pasted, deleted, moved, etc. Again, whatever changes you make are local to the Project file and will have no impact on the original computer files.

Visualizing your Project

Consider this an overall picture of how a project can evolve:

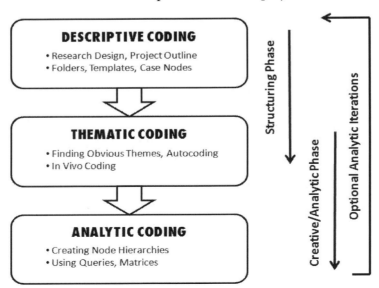

Exploring this Book

This book begins by describing the system requirements for NVivo for Mac. Chapter 2 describes how NVivo's user interface is designed and basic settings for optimizing your software. Chapter 3 explains how to create, save and backup your NVivo Project file.

Chapters 4 - 8 cover how to import, create and edit text, audio, video, and picture data. Chapter 9 outlines how to create Memos and Links. Chapters 10 - 12 explain Nodes, Classifications and Coding—the lifeblood of qualitative data analysis with NVivo. Chapters 13 and 14 discuss creating Queries, saving them and creating Nodes from Query results.

Chapter 15 deals with NVivo's powerful functionality to support literature reviews and bibliographic data.

Chapter 16 moves into managing surveys and questionnaires, called Datasets in NVivo.

Chapter 17 describes capturing data from the web and social media and Chapter 18 about capturing data from the cloud-service OneNote.

Chapter 19 deals with important aspects of collaboration using NVivo when you are a part of a research team.

Chapter 20 describe how to graphically illustrate a project using Maps, Charts and Diagrams.

Finally, Chapter 21 reviews the help functions available in NVivo for Mac, and Chapter 22 contains our glossary.

Graphic Conventions

In this book we have applied some simple graphic conventions with the intention of improving readability:

Convention	Example	Comment
Commands	Go to **Data | Import | Documents**	Ribbon menu **Data** and Menu group **Import** and Menu option **Documents**
Menus	Go to **File → Options**	Main menu and options with **Bold**
Mouse functions	Right-click and select **New Query → Text Search**	Right-click with the mouse and select menu and sub-menu with **Bold**
Dialog box Tabs	Select the **Audio/Video** tab	Optional tabs with **Bold**
Functions	Select *Advanced Find* from **Options** drop-down list	Variable with **Bold**, the value with *Italic*; Heading with **Bold**, options with *Italic*
Buttons	Confirm with [**OK**]	Graphical buttons within brackets
Keyboard commands	Use the [**Del**] key to delete	Key is written within brackets
Typing	Type `Bibliography` in the textbox	`Courier` for text to be typed
Text	..`[1-3]` is shown in the textbox	`Courier` for shown text
Keyboard shortcuts	.. key command [**Shift**] + [⌘] + [**E**]	Hold the first (and second) key while touching the last

Before you Install NVivo for Mac

Installation is made in two steps: first, the 'installation', which requires a license key and second the 'activation' which requires online or telephone authentication.

Should you need to change your computer, remember to deactivate your license **before** you uninstall NVivo in the old machine. Then you can reinstall NVivo in the new computer with your license key followed by a new activation procedure.

System Requirements – Minimum
- Mac computer with an Intel Core 2 Duo, Core i3, Core i5, Core i7, or Xeon processor
- Mac OS X 10.9 (Mavericks) or later
- 2 GB of RAM (as defined by the Mac OS X Mavericks minimum requirements)
- 1280 x 800 screen resolution or higher
- 2 GB of available disk space - or more depending on data storage needs

System Requirements – Recommended
- Mac computer with an Intel Core i5, Core i7, or Xeon processor
- Mac OS X 10.9 (Mavericks) or later
- 4 GB RAM or more
- 1440 x 900 screen resolution or higher
- 4GB SSD of available disk space - or more depending on data storage needs
- Internet Connection
- Google Chrome 44 or later (required for NCapture—a browser extension that allows you to gather material from the web)

Handling Other File Formats

Converting between different NVivo for Mac project file formats follows the principle that a later NVivo for Mac version can convert earlier formats to current format, but not vice versa.

Many other conversion procedures are instead incorporated in NVivo 11 (Windows). The conversion takes place when such file is selected for opening with NVivo 11 or when NVivo 11 intends to import such file into its project.

In some cases NVivo will ask for certain software for the conversion and may suggest direct download with a link.

File formats presently possible to convert are:
- Earlier versions of NVivo
- NVivo for Mac
- Atlas.ti
- MAXQDA

Atlas.ti and MAXQDA are subject to restrictions depending on software versions and releases. When you are considering such conversions, you are welcome to contact support@formkunskap.com

Furthermore, NVivo 11 (Windows) can also save its native file format to NVivo for Mac format but some project items that do not exist in the Mac version will be lost.

2. THE NVIVO INTERFACE

This chapter is about the architecture of the NVivo screen. A work session usually starts in the Navigation View with a selection of a heading and the opening of a folder. In the List View you select the a certain Project Item. The Detail View is populated when you open a Project Item and can study that item's content.

Project work is done through the ribbon menus, keyboard commands or via the menu options brought up by right-clicking your mouse.

Tip: We suggest simply opening your NVivo software and experimenting with the interface. Challenging yourself to play around in NVivo is a great way to learn!

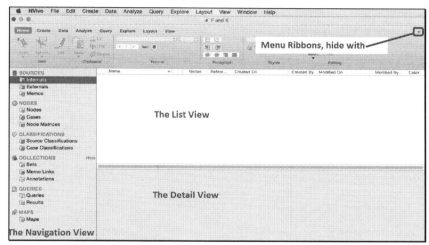

You will soon find that the NVivo screen has two menu alternatives, the Mac style menus and the Ribbon style menus. To some extent the two alternatives menus have the same options, but some are unique for the Mac style menu. The **Home** button is unique for the ribbon style menu:

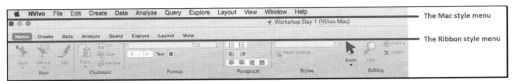

The Mac style menu has the following specific menu alternatives: , **NVivo**, **File**, **Edit**, **Window** and **Help**.

The other menu options are identical with those in the Ribbon Style menu.

In the Mac style menu you will find the following unique options:

Menu	Functions
	The wellknown Mac system commands
NVivo	About NVivo, Preferences..., Licensing, Check for Updates, Hide NVivo and Quit NVivo
File	New Project, Open Project, Compact Project, Close, Save, Project Properties
Edit	Formatting commands
Window	Is described below
Help	Is described in Chapter 21

This is the **Window** option from the Mac style menu:

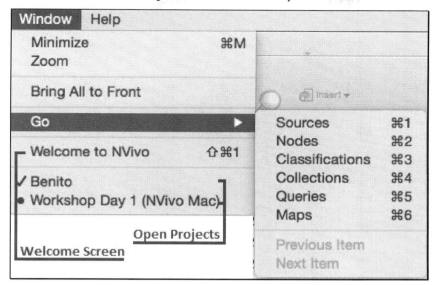

The direct navigation keystrokes under **Go** relate to the following commands:

[⌘] + [1] equals 'Under **SOURCES** open **Internals** folder'

[⌘] + [2] equals 'Under **NODES** open **Nodes** folder'

[⌘] + [3] equals 'Under **CLASSIFICATIONS** open **Source Classifications** folder'

[⌘] + [4] equals 'Under **COLLECTIONS** open **Sets** folder'

[⌘] + [5] equals 'Under **QUERIES** open **Queries** folder'

[⌘] + [6] equals 'Under **MAPS** open **Maps** folder'

These are the default folders and are valid when you create a new project or when you open an existing one. During ongoing work sessions, the keystrokes open folders or subfolders last opened under respective heading.

The Navigation View & Folders

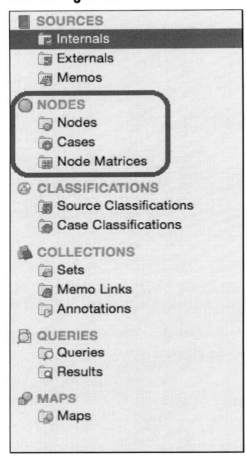

The Navigation View contains headings and a number of default folders that have non-editabe names. These folders can only contain specific functional items. Some of them, but not all, can also have subfolders in several levels. Such user-defined folders are also shown in the Navigation View.

Our instructions in this book follow two syntax principles:
- We refer to the *Ribbon style* menu where applicable
- We write:
'Under **NODES** open **Cases** or any of its subfolders'
The headings like **NODES** are not folders but **Nodes**, **Cases** and **Node Matrices** are.

- The Virtual Explorer

Each Navigation heading contains a number of folders where relevant Project Items are stored. The folders associated with each Navigation Button are displayed in the Virtual Explorer, Area 2.

Virtual file paths are called Hierarchical Names. Only folders and Nodes have hierarchical names in NVivo. In the NVivo environment, hierarchical names are written with a double backslash between folders and a single backslash between a Node and its child Node.

For example:

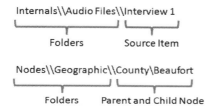

> **Did you know?** NVivo folders are called *virtual folders* as opposed to folders in a Windows environment. NVivo folders are *virtual* because they exist only in the NVivo project file. In most cases, *Virtual folders* perform like any Windows folder - you can create sub-folders, drag and drop project items into allowable folders, copy and paste folders. Certain folders are predefined in the NVivo project template and cannot be changed or deleted whereas other folders can be created by the user.

Creating a New Folder

NVivo contains a core set of template folders that cannot be deleted or moved. Users can create new subfolders under some of these template folders: **Internals, Externals, Memos, Nodes, Cases, Sets, Queries**, and **Maps**:

1. Under **SOURCES, NODES** or **QUERIES** open one of the default folders.
2. Go to **Create | Collections | Folder** or right-click and select **New Folder....**

For each new folder, the **Folder Properties** dialog box appears:

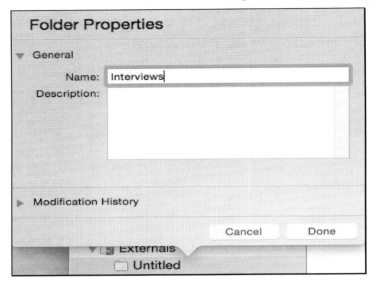

3   Type a name (compulsory) and a description (optional), then [**Done**].

When creating more subfolders at lower levels, open any folder and follow again the above instruction. You can build any folder structure you like.

Renaming a Folder
Select a folder, right-click and select **Get Info** and the **Folder Properties** dialog box will show. Rename and click [**Done**].

Deleting a Folder
Deleting a folder also deletes its subfolders and all contents thereunder.

1   Select the folder or folders that you want to delete.
2   Go to **Home | Editing | Delete**
    or right-click and select **Delete**
    or use the [⬅] key.
3   Confirm with [**OK**].

The List View

The List View is similar to any list of files, but NVivo calls these Project Items within an Item List.

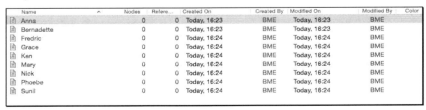

22

Item Properties

All items have certain characteristics that can be changed or updated through the item's properties menu:
1. Select the item in the List View that you want to change, rename or update.
2. Go to **Home | Item | Get Info**
   or right-click and select **Get Info**

An item properties dialog box (in this case, **Document Properties**) may look like this:

All information in this dialog box is editable. When done confirm with **[Done]**. Regarding the section Attribute Values see Chapter 11, page 107.

Colors

Source items, Nodes, Cases, Attribute values and users can be assigned colors. Colors serve as visual cues for project researchers and as a result they can be used for a number of reasons. Most importantly, a color assigned to a Node will be visually represented in coding stripes (see page 125). NVivo has seven pre-defined colors and an item's color marking is shown in the List View.

1. Select the item or items (without opening) that you want to color mark.
2. Go to **Home | Item | Get Info → Color → <select>**
   or right-click and select **Color → <select>**.

Classifying an Item

All Source Items and Case Nodes can be classified, NVivo's term for associating project data with some form of metadata. Although we discuss Classifications further in Chapter 11, we want to signal that working with item classifications can take place in the List View.

1. Select the item or items that you want to classify.
2. Go to **Home | Item | Get Info → Classification → <select>**
   or right-click and select **Classification → <select>**.

Sorting Options for a List

In the same way Mac's Finder allows file lists to be sorted according to file name or file type, etc., NVivo for Mac offers several ways to sort project items in a list.

1. Display a list of items in the List View.
2. Go to **Layout | Sort & Filter | Sort by → <select>**.
   or place the cursor below the list, right-click and select **Sort by → <select>**.

The options offered depend on of the type of items in the list.

You can also use the column heads for sorting. Sorting by commands or sorting with column heads always adds a small triangle to the column head in question. Clicking again on this column head turns the sorting in the opposite order:

Name	Sources	Refere...	Created On	Created By	Modified On	Modified By
Defining volunteer work	1	1	29 Nov 2015 15:15	BME	29 Nov 2015 15:16	BME
Family Values	12	77	16 Feb 2016 18:46	BME	16 Feb 2016 18:53	BME
Family Values 2	9	64	16 Feb 2016 18:50	BME	16 Feb 2016 18:54	BME
▼ Reasons for Volunteering	12	279	29 Nov 2015 12:01	BME	29 Nov 2015 12:02	BME
Family Values	12	79	29 Nov 2015 10:08	BME	16 Feb 2016 18:55	BME
Motivation	12	103	29 Nov 2015 10:22	BME	29 Nov 2015 10:23	BME
Payments	12	42	29 Nov 2015 10:27	BME	29 Nov 2015 10:28	BME
Satisfaction	12	55	29 Nov 2015 10:30	BME	29 Nov 2015 10:31	BME
Untitled	1	8	4 Jul 2016 09:45	BME	4 Jul 2016 09:45	BME
Untitled (2)	1	1	4 Jul 2016 09:48	BME	4 Jul 2016 09:48	BME

Exporting the Item List
Exporting your item list is also possible:
1. Go to **Data | Export | List...**
   or place the cursor below the list, right-click and select **Export...**
2. Select file format, location and name, then [**OK**].

The file formats are .DOC, DOCX, .TXT or .ODT.

Deleting an Item
You can delete items from the List View. When you delete a parent Node you also delete its child Nodes. Likewise, deleting a Classification also deletes its Attributes.
1. Select the appropriate folder or its subfolder.
2. Select the item or items that you want to delete.
3. Go to **Home | Editing | Delete**
   or right-click and select **Delete**
   or use the [←] key.
4. Confirm with [**Delete**].

The Detail View
The below image is an example of an open Project Item in Detail View, which can include documents, audio clips, videos, pictures, memos, or Nodes

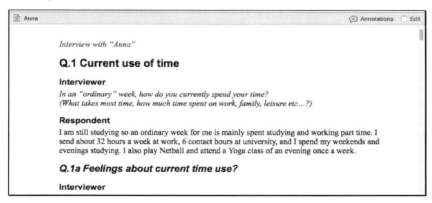

Each time a Source Item is opened it is Read Only. The document is made instantly editable by checking the *Edit* link at the top right of an open item. Alternatively, you can go to **Home | Item | Edit** which is a toggling function.

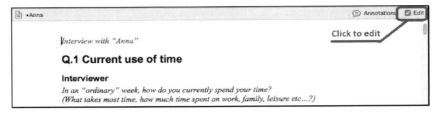

The Info Bar of the Detail View
When any project item is opened in the Detail View, there is an info bar in the lower section like this:

Where **SOURCES** is a heading from the Navigation View and **Internals** and **Interviews** are folders and **Sunil** is a source item.

This corresponds to the previously mentioned syntax:
Internals\\Interviews\\Sunil

Closing an Item in Detail View
You can open several project items and each of them are listed at the left lower corner of the screen. Pointing at one such name brings forward corresponding item. When you want to close all such open windows point at the **[OPEN ITEMS]**, right-click and select *Close All*. When you want to close one such window, point at the name of the item, and click the checkmark **[X]**.

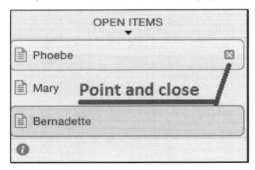

An alternative to Close All is go to **View | Application | Close All**.

> **Did you know?** Read Only mode doesn't mean that a project item is *locked* from making changes. You can still code and create links (but not hyperlinks) in a Read Only Source Item.

Copying, Cutting, and Pasting

Standard Mac conventions for copying, cutting and pasting text and images prevail in NVivo. In addition, NVivo can also copy and paste complete Project Items like documents, memos, Nodes, etc. However, it is not possible to paste Nodes into folders meant for documents and vice versa (this would breach the software's folder template conventions). It is only possible to paste an item into the folder appropriate for that type of folder (e.g., paste a Node within the Nodes folder, a Query within the Queries folder, etc.). To copy and paste within NVivo:

1. Go to **Home | Clipboard | Copy**
   or right-click and select **Copy**
   or [⌘] + [C].
2. Select the appropriate folder or parent Node under which you want to place the item.
3. Go to **Home | Clipboard | Paste**
   or right-click and select **Paste**
   or [⌘] + [V].

Cutting with **Home | Clipboard | Cut** or right-click and select **Cut** or [⌘] + [X] applies to text in Edit mode.

Cutting project items is implemented by Drag-and-Drop provided that the target location accepts the kind of item that is dropped.

Working with Sets
You'll find Sets in the folder **Sets** under the heading **COLLECTIONS**. Sets are customizable groups of shortcuts to selected Source Items, Nodes and Cases. A Set is a subset or a collection of Project Item shortcuts that allow you to access customized groups of items without moving or copying them from their original locations.
1. Under **COLLECTIONS** open **Sets** folder.
2. Right-click and select **New Set...**
   or place the cursor in any empy space in the List View, right-click and select **New Set...**

The dislog box **Set Properties** appears.

3. In the **Set Properties** dialog box type a name (compulsory) and a descrption (optionally) of your new **Set**.
4. Confirm with [**Done**].

Next, you need to allocate the members to your set:
1. Select the item or items that will be allocated to one of your sets.
2. Right-click select **Add To Set...**

This dialog box appears:

3. Select a set and confirm with [**Select**].

You can also select item or items and create a new Set.
1. Select an item or items that will form a new set.
2. Go to **Create As → Set...**

The **Set Properties** dialog box is shown.

3   Type a name (compulsory) and a description (optionally) of the new set.
4   Confirm with [**Done**].

> **Sets** are a powerful organizational tools in NVivo, but beginners and intermediate users are sometimes confused by their functionality. The main function of Sets is to allow users the flexibility of organizing certain project items into virtual groups.
>
> For example, we are involved in a project involving interview data, focus group data, writing samples, and social media data for a group of 20 undergraduate social science students. As a team, we could organize these data sources according to type of data source (e.g., an interview folder, a focus group folder, etc.) or we could organize these data sources according to student (e.g., a folder for Student 1, a folder for Student 2, etc.). While each method of organization has its merits, Sets allows us to organize project items according to type of data source *and* create a Set organizing data sources according to student. As alternative methods of organizing text items present themselves, more and more sets can be generated.

Ribbon Tabs

Commands are organized into logical groups, collected together under tabs. Each tab relates to a type of activity, such as creating new Project Items or analyzing your source materials.

The tabs are **Home**, **Create**, **Data**, **Analyze**, **Query**, **Explore**, **Layout**, and **View**. Within each tab, related commands are grouped together. For example, the **Format** group on the **Home** tab contains commands for setting font size, type, bold, italics and underline.

The ribbon is optimized for a screen resolution of 1280 by 1024 pixels, when the NVivo window is maximized on your screen.

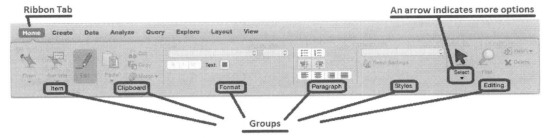

Command example: Go to Home | Editing | Select → Select All

The **Home** tab provides commands related to formatting (e.g., paragraph styles) and workflow (e.g., cut and paste):

The **Create** tab provides commands related to making new Project Items (e.g., creating a new Node):

The **Data** tab provides commands related to importing and exporting Project Items:

The **Analyze** tab provides commands related to coding, linking, and annotating:

The **Query** tab provides commands related to searching and querying your data.

The **Explore** tab provides commands related to analytic representations.

The **Layout** tab provides commands related to list views and tables:

The **View** tab provides commands related to visual aspects of the Project Item interface (e.g. coding stripes):

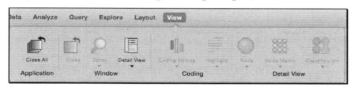

Application Preferences

NVivo project settings can be adjusted for an individual project or for the NVivo software overall. **Application Preferences** adjust settings for the software overall, and some changes you make only apply to new projects and will therefore have an effect on the **Project Properties** (see page 39) settings for future projects:
1   Go to **NVivo → Preferences...**
    or [⌘] + [,]

The [**Revert**] button will change the options back to the default settings and cannot be undone. Your username and initials will be preserved.

The General Tab

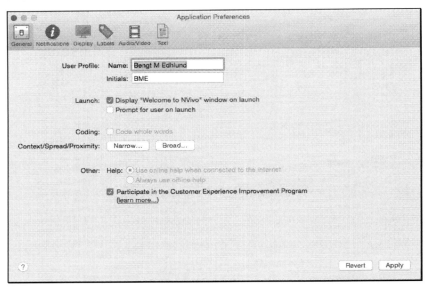

The **General** tab contains default options for working with the NVivo interface such as User Profile. You can change User profile any time during a work session. Coding properties like the defintions of Narrow and Broad spreading is made here.

You can set Display Welcome to NVivo and/or Prompt for user on launch.

Settings made here take immediate effect in an ongoing project and will also become default for new projects.

Confirm changes with [**Apply**].

The Notifications Tab

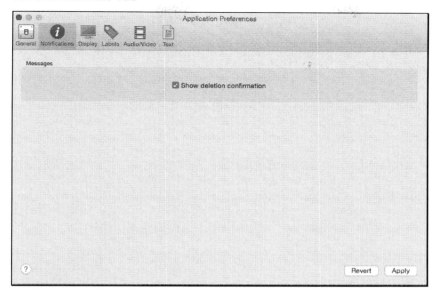

The **Notifications** tab allows you to select Show deletion confirmation.

Settings under this tab take immediate effect on an ongoing project.

Confirm changes with [**Apply**].

The Display Tab

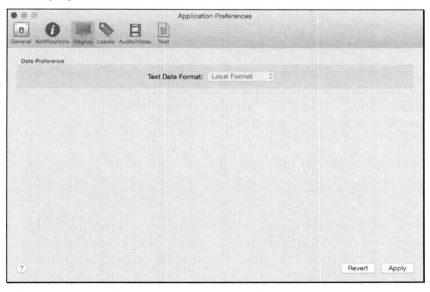

The **Display** tab contains no setting options at present.
Confirm changes with [**Apply**].

The Labels Tab

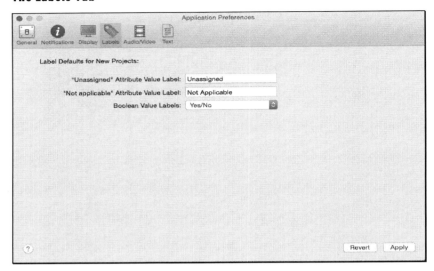

The **Labels** tab allows you to customize the names of Attribute Values and the Boolean Value Labels.

Settings made here are inherited to new projects. Changes in current projects are made in **Project Properties, Labels** tab (see page 41).

Confirm changes with [**Apply**].

The Audio/Video Tab

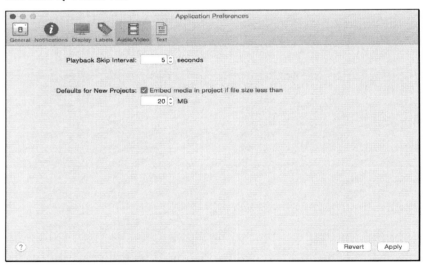

The **Audio/Video** tab contains settings for the skip interval for skipping forward and skipping backward. The threshold value for embedding is set here. Max value is 40 MB. These settings have an effect on new projects.

Confirm changes with [**Apply**].

The Text Tab

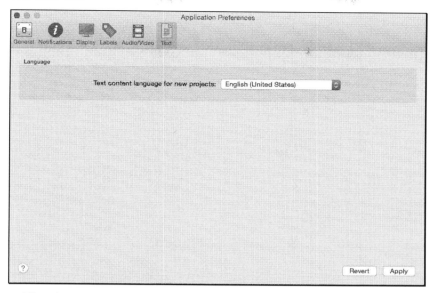

The **Text** tab allows you to make settings for the content language that you want to use. The setting of language does not have an effect on the ongoing project. For the next new project the chosen language will be default. If you want to change content language for the current project go to the **General** tab of **Project Properties** dialog box (see page 39).

The supported languages are: Chinese (PRC), English (UK), English (US), French, German, Japanese, Portuguese and Spanish. If you use any other language then you can set the language as *Other*.

The chosen content language has an impact on the current stop word list. See further under the **General** tab of **Project Properties** dialog box (see page 39).

Confirm changes with [**Apply**].

Alternate Screen Layouts

Sharing the screen with three windows can sometimes be confusing. But NVivo offers an alternate screen layout to split the screen space vertically instead of horizontally between the List View and the Detail View.

1. Go to **View | Window | Detail View → On Right**.

The On Right Detail View is very handy when coding with drag-and-drop (see page 119).

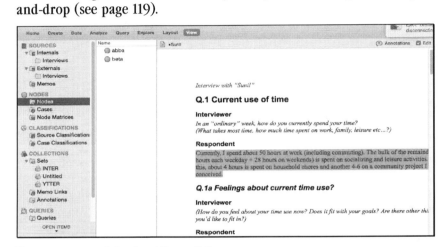

To revert to original setting of the screen:

1. Go to **View | Window | Detail View → At Bottom**.

New to NVivo, your **Detail View** setting preference can now be saved in between sessions.

3. BEGINNING YOUR PROJECT

An NVivo project is a term used for all source documents and other items that altogether form a qualitative study. Importantly, a project is also a computer file that houses all those Project Items.

NVivo can open and process several projects at a time. When several project are open you will find open projects listed under the **Window** menu, see page 19. Cut, copy, and paste between two such program windows is limited to text, graphics and images and not Project Items like documents or Nodes.

A project is built up of several items with different properties. There are internal sources (i.e., documents, memos), external sources (i.e., web sites), Nodes and queries.

Creating a New Project

The Welcome screen will greet you each time you launch NVivo, and it is from here that you have the option to create a new project file:

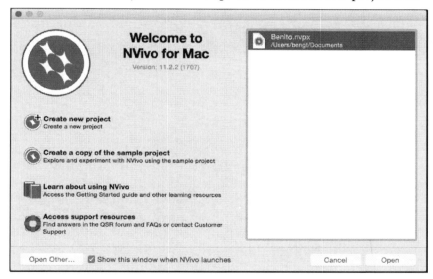

Your most recent projects are listed in the right box on the Welcome screen. You can also create a new project while navigating inside an existing project:

1 Go to **File → New Project** or [⌘] + [N].

The **New Project** dialog box appears:

You must type a name for your project file, but the description is optional. Select a location for your project file. The preferred location for ongoing project files is the native harddisk, the C-disk.

The name of a project can later be changed without changing the file name. Finally confirm with [**Create**].

Sources & Project Size

NVivo is capable of importing and creating a variety of file types as data (e.g., text sources, tables, images, video, PDFs, etc.) Collectively, these items care called *Sources*. We'll discuss sources at length over the next few chapters, but for now it's important you understand that NVivo can either *import* Sources to a project file or *link* Sources externally to a Project file.

Files that are imported into NVivo are amalgamated by the software, which means that they become a part of the NVivo project. These are called Internal Sources. For example, any changes you make to imported sources (e.g., a text Source) are not reflected in the original document (e.g., a Microsoft Word text file).

Files that are linked into NVivo are only referenced by the software, which means that they exist independently of the NVivo project. These are called External Sources and cannot be coded, only the external item (the text inside NVivo) can be coded.

Audio- and video files are special as they can either be embedded or remain stored outside NVivo. If such files remain outside NVivo they can still be handled as if they were embedded, that is you can link and code, etc. Therefore, even not embedded media files are Internal Sources. It is the size of such files that decides if it should be embedded or not. A threshold value set by the user decides. The threshold value however, cannot exceed 40 MB (see page 34).

An NVivo for Mac Project file size is maximum 512 GB. However, the observable project file size is dependent on machine specifications and type of project data. NVivo for Mac projects are able to handle up thousands of sources including documents, audio and video items. Large Project Items (e.g., audio and video files) can be stored outside the project file. Linking to external files allows you to keep the project file size down.

Project Properties

When a new project is created some settings from the **Application Options** dialog box are inherited. This dialog box opens by going to **File → Project Properties**, and the settings that are inherited are found under these tabs: **Labels** and **Audio/Video**. Modifications and templates which are made in the **Project Properties** dialog box are only valid for your current project:

1. Go to **File → Project Properties**
   or [**Shift**] + [⌘] + [,].

The [**Cancel**]-button reverts to previously saved settings.

Event Log

In the leftmost corner of the NVivo screen there is an Info symbol: 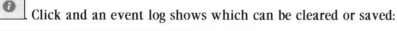. Click and an event log shows which can be cleared or saved:

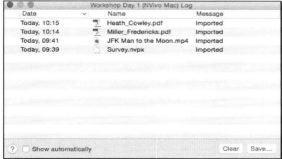

The General Tab

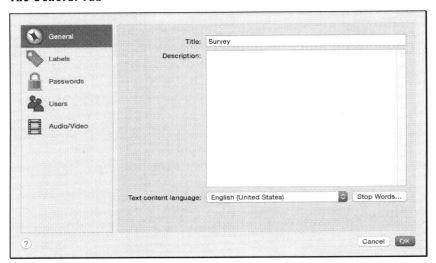

In this dialog box it is possible to modify your project name, but not the NVivo project file name. From the **Text content language** drop-down list you will, if available, select the language of the data used in the project, otherwise select English or Other. Your content language will be the default language for Text Search Queries and Word Frequency Queries. For all languages except Other a default stop word list is built in. The stop words list can be edited using the [**Stop Words**] button or while using Word Frequency Queries (see Chapter 13, Queries). Such customized stop word lists are only valid for the current project. Even when the content language setting is Other you can build a customized stop word list.

Tip: Your stop words list can be edited with the button [**Stop Words**]. Remember, customized stop words are only valid for the current project.

The Description (max 512 characters) can be modified.

Confirm changes with [**OK**].

The Labels Tab

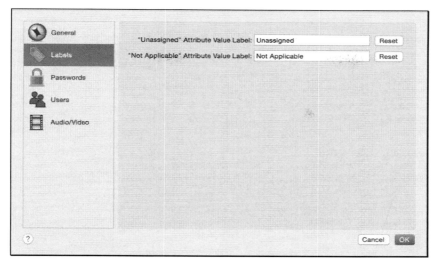

Under the **Labels** tab you can change some of your project's 'labels'. The **[Reset]** buttons reset to the values defined in the **Application Options** dialog box, under the **Labels** tab (see page 34).

Confirm changes with **[OK]**.

The Passwords Tab

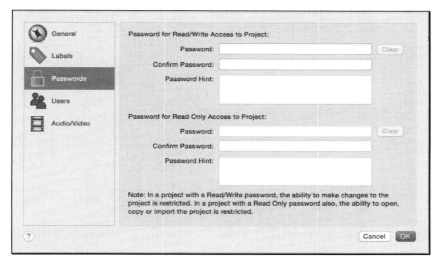

Under the **Passwords** tab you can define separate passwords for opening and editing your current project.

Confirm changes with **[OK]**.

The Users Tab

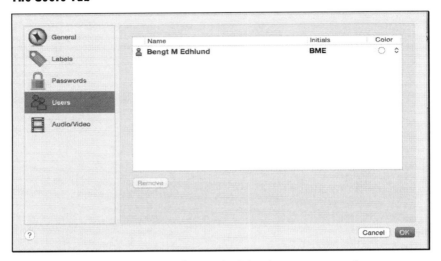

All users who have actively worked in the current project are listed here. The current user is identified by bold letters. You can replace a user with someone else on the list by selecting the user who shall be replaced (triangle) and using the [**Remove**] button. Select who will replace the deleted user by selecting from the list of users.

Users can also be given an individual color marking. Use the drop-down list in the Color column and select color.

Confirm changes with [**OK**].

The Audio/Video Tab

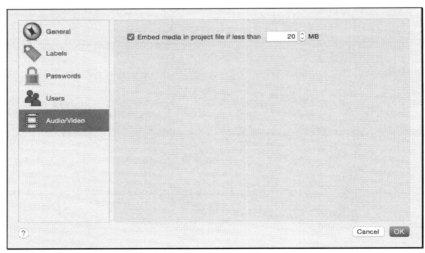

The settings for new projects are inherited from the **Application Options** dialog box, the **Audio/Video** tab (see page 34). Modifications made here are only valid for the current project.

Confirm changes with [**OK**].

Merging Projects

Projects can be merged by importing one project to another:
1. Open the project into which you wish to import a project.
2. Go to **Data | Import | Project**.

This dialog box appears:

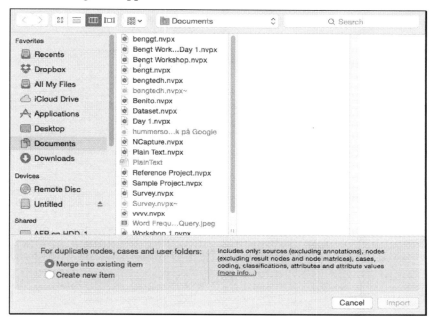

3. Select the project file to be imported.
4. Select the item options that you need for the import.
5. Confirm with [**Import**].

As a confirmation an Import Project Results Report is displayed.

N.B. The import project function in NVivo for Mac does not import Queries, the Results folder, Node Matrices, Annotations and Sets.

Tip: Merging projects is a useful function for teams collaborating on the same project. Users can independently make changes to their project and, later, import their changes into a project 'master' file.

Exporting Project Data

All Project Items (except folders) can be exported in various file formats. For example, project Memos can be created in NVivo and then exported as .DOC files for sharing with others:
1. Open a project and select an item or items from the List View.
2. Go to **Data | Export | Items**.
3. Select the appropriate file format.
4. Confirm with [**OK**].

Saving Projects

You can save the project file at any time during a work session. The complete project is saved; it is not possible to save single Project Items. We recommend saving manually frequently to make sure your data is secured.

    1   Go to **File → Save**
         or [⌘] + [S].

Compact a Project

Over time, NVivo project data can become fragmented. If you are working with a large project, data fragmentation can cause problems in NVivo. To ensure optimal performance, you should compact your project on a regular basis.

    1   Close the project you want to compact.
    2   Start NVivo but you need not open any project.
    3   Go to **File → Compress Project...**
    4   Select the project you want to Compress.
    5   Finish with [**Compress**].

Closing NVivo

After each work session save your project file and close NVivo. Close with:

    1   Go to **File → Close**
         or [⌘] + [**W**].

4. HANDLING TEXT SOURCES

From interview transcripts to government white papers, text data makes up the majority of qualitative research data. Text items can be easily imported from files created outside NVivo, like Word documents or any text file formats. Text items can also be created by NVivo as most word processing tools and functions are incorporated in NVivo software, which we'll discuss in the next chapter. Handling PDF documents is dealt with later on in this book.

Importing Documents

This section is about text-based sources that can be imported and these file types are: .DOC, .DOCX, .RTF, and .TXT. When text files are imported into NVivo, they become Project Items under the heading **SOURCES**:

1. Go to **Data | Import | Documents**
   Default folder is **Internals**
   Go to 4.

alternatively

1. Under **SOURCES** open **Internals** or any of its subfolders.
2. Go to **Data | Import | Documents**
   Go to 4.

alternatively

2. Click on any empty space in the List View.
3. Right-click and select **Import → Documents...**
   Go to 4.

alternatively

3. Drag and drop your file's icon from an outside folder into the List View.
   Go to 4.

In each case, the following dialog box appears:

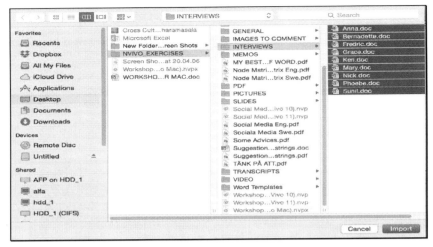

4   This dialog gives you all options to navigate your computer and select the document or documents that you want to import. Finally confirm with [**Import**].

When only one document has been imported, the **Document Properties** dialog box appears:

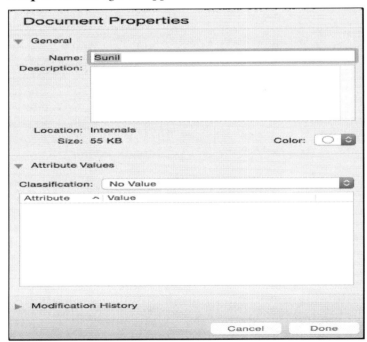

This dialog box will make it possible to modify the name of the item and optionally add a description.

5   Confirm with [**Done**].

Here is a typical List View of some document items:

Name	Nodes	Refere...	Created On	Created By
Anna	0	0	11 Jun 2016 16:23	BME
Bernadette	0	0	11 Jun 2016 16:23	BME
Fredric	0	0	11 Jun 2016 16:24	BME
Grace	0	0	11 Jun 2016 16:24	BME
Ken	0	0	11 Jun 2016 16:24	BME
Mary	0	0	11 Jun 2016 16:24	BME
Nick	0	0	11 Jun 2016 16:24	BME
Phoebe	0	0	11 Jun 2016 16:24	BME
Sunil	2	2	11 Jun 2016 16:24	BME

Creating a New Document

You can also create your own text items within NVivo, much the same as creating a Word document.

1. Under **SOURCES** open **Internals** or any of its subfolders.
2. Go to **Create | Sources | Document**.
   Go to 4.

alternatively

2. Click on any empty space in the List View.
3. Right-click and select **New Internal → Document...**

The **Document Properties** dialog box as shown above will appear.

4. Type a name (compulsory) and a description (optionally), then [**OK**].

The text area opens and new documents are opened in edit mode.

Opening a Document

Now that you have imported or created a list of Source Items, you can easily open one or more items anytime you see fit:

1. Under **SOURCES** open **Internals** or any of its subfolders.
2. Select the document that you want to open.
3. Go to **Home | Item | Open**
   or right-click and select **Open**
   or double-click on the document.

Please note, NVivo only allows you to open one document at a time, but several documents can stay open simultaneously.

Exporting a Document

As mentioned, you may wish at some point to export a text Source Item, such as a Memo you wrote inside NVivo but now need to email to a collaborator.

1. Under **SOURCES** open **Internals** or any of its subfolders.
2. Select the document or documents that you want to export.
3. Go to **Data | Export | Items**
   or right-click and select **Export...**

The following dialog box appears:

4. Decide file location, and file type. Possible file types are: .DOCX, .DOC, .TXT or .ODT. Confirm with **[OK]**.

Remember, coding made on text items cannot be transferred when a Source Item is exported.

External Items

For any number of reasons, you may wish to refer to external items outside of your NVivo project (i.e., a web site, a file too large or a file type that is incompatible). NVivo allows you to create external items that can act as placeholders or links.

Creating an External Item
    1   Go to **Create | Sources | External**.
        Default folder is **Externals**.
        Go to 3.

alternatively
    1   Under **SOURCES** open **Externals**.or any of its subfolders.
    2   Go to **Create | Sources | External**
        or right-click and select **New External...**

The **External Properties** dialog box appears:

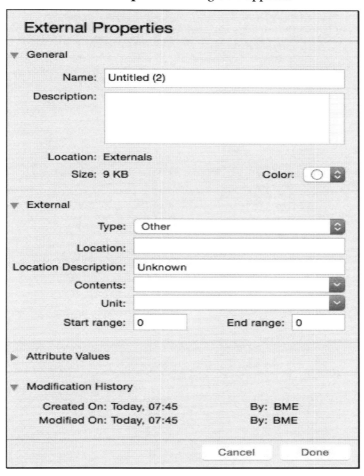

3   Type name (compulsory) and description (optional), then go to the External section.
    At **Type** select *File link* and then use the [⊙] button to find the target file. Alternatively, at Type select *Web link* and type or paste the URL in the text box below.
4   Confirm with [**Done**].

This is a typical list view of some external items:

Name	Nodes	Refere...	Created On	Created By	Modified On	Modified By	Color
A pilot Study	0	0	Today, 07:59	BME	Today, 08:00	BME	
An Online Corse	0	0	Today, 07:44	BME	Today, 08:00	BME	
Attitudes of Female Nurses	0	0	Today, 08:00	BME	Today, 08:01	BME	

Opening an External Item

External items act identical to internal items within NVivo's Sources folder: they can contain text and that text can be edited and coded. To open an external item for viewing or editing:
1   Under **SOURCES** open **Externals** or any of its subfolders.
2   Select the external item that you want to open.
3   Go to **Home | Item | Open**
    or right-click and select **Open**
    or double-click on the external item.

Remember, NVivo can only open one external item at a time, but several items can stay open simultaneously.

Opening an External Source

Unlike internal items, external items are necessarily linked to external sources, which can be opened through NVivo:
1   Under **SOURCES** open **Externals** or any of its subfolders.
2   Select the external item that has a link to the external file or URL that you want to open.
3   Right-click and select **Open External File**.

Editing an External Source or Link

1   Under **SOURCES** open **Externals** or any of its subfolders.
2   Select the external item that you want to edit.
3   Go to **Home | Item | Get Info**
    or right-click and select **Get Info**.

The **External Properties** dialog box appears.
4   Select the **External** section and if you want to link to a new target file use [⊙]. If you want to modify a web link change the URL.

Exporting an External Item

Similar to internal items, external items can be exported. However, the linked external file or the web link is not included in the exported item, only the external item text contents are exported.

    1   Under **SOURCES** open **Externals** or any of its subfolders.
    2   Select the external item or items that you want to export.
    3   Go to **Data | Export | Items**
         or right-click and select **Export...**

This dialog box appears:

    4   Decide file name, file location, and file type. Possible file types are: .DOCX, .DOC, .TXT or .ODT. Confirm with [**OK**].

5. EDITING TEXT IN NVIVO

Whether you import a text document or create a new one, NVivo contains most of the functions of modern word processing software. Notwithstanding the fact that text document files are often imported, understanding how to edit text in NVivo is useful. Aside from its ability to edit existing source documents, you can use NVivo's word processing functionality to compose any Source item like Memos and Externals.

Formatting Text

Remember, each time a Source Item is opened it is Read-Only. Therefore, check *Edit* (or **Home | Item | Edit**) at the top right of a Source Item before editing is possible.

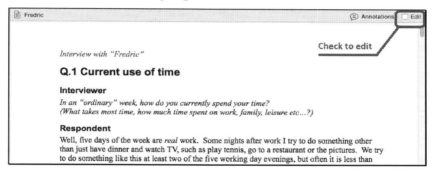

Selecting the whole document:
1. Position the cursor anywhere in the document.
2. Go to **Home | Editing | Select→ Select All** or [⌘] + [A] or right-click and select **Select All**.

You can also select any paragraph like his:
1. Position the cursor in the current paragraph.
2. Triple-click with the mouse.

> **Tip: Selecting Text**
> Select a passage of text by holding left-click and mousing over it. Double left-clicking on a single word highlights just that word. And did you know that triple left-clicking on a single word selects the whole paragraph? Both of these shortcuts can be useful when coding.

Changing Fonts, Font Style, Size, and Color
1. Select the text you want to format.
2. Go to **Home | Format → Font...**
3. Select the options you need with immediate effect.

Selecting a Style
1. Position the cursor in the paragraph you want to format.
2. Go to **Home | Styles**.
3. Select from the list of styles you need with immediate effect.

Aligning Paragraphs

Selecting Alignments
1. Position the cursor in the paragraph you want to format.
2. Go to **Home | Paragraph**.
3. Select from the list of alignment options.

Selecting Indentation
1. Position the cursor in the paragraph for which you want to change the indentation.
2. Go to **Home | Paragraph**.
3. Select increased or decreased indentation.

Creating Lists
1. Select the paragraphs that you want to make as a list.
2. Go to **Home | Paragraph**.
3. Select a bulleted or numbered list.

Finding and Navigating Text

Finding Text
1. Open a document.
2. Go to **Home | Editing | Find**.

The **search** box appears:

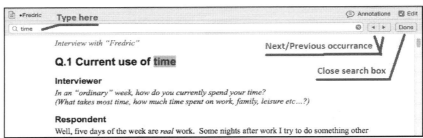

3. Type a search word, then click **Next/Previous**.

Selecting Text

- Selecting text: Click and drag
- Selecting one word: Double-click
- Selecting a paragraph:
    1. Position the cursor in the paragraph you want to select.
    2. Triple-click with the mouse.
- Selecting the whole document:
    1. Position the cursor anywhere in the document.
    2. Go to **Home | Editing | Select→ Select All**
       or [⌘] + [A].

Inserting Images and Dates

Inserting an Image
1. Position the cursor where you want to insert an image.
2. Go to **Home | Editing | Insert → Image...**
3. Select an image with the file browser. Only .BMP, .JPG and .GIF file formats can be inserted.
4. Confirm with [**Open**].

Inserting Date and Time (presently not implemented)
1. Position the cursor where you want to insert date and time.
2. Go to **Home | Editing | Insert → Date/Time**
   or [**Shift**] + [⌘] + [**T**].

Zooming

The native Mac zooming options are applicable. One of the easiest methods is using the [⌘]-key and the mouse wheel.

About Printing from NVivo

Printing and previewing is currently not implemented in the current version of NVivo for Mac. Instead all project items can be exported to various external file formats. That means that any third party software will take care of its own printing options.

Tip: NVivo is powerful software for organizing and analyzing text documents, but it is weak as a standalone word processor. A best practice we recommend is creating a document in Word (or your preferref word processing software) and then importing the text into NVivo.

Tip: Make it a PDF!
In the event you find NVivo is mishandling your document formatting, try converting your text document to a PDF. NVivo is also a powerful tool for handling PDF files with special formatting, like multiple columns. What about if you want to import a PowerPoint presentation into NVivo? Make it a PDF!

Limitations in Editing Documents in NVivo

NVivo has certain limitations in creating advanced formatted documents.

Some of these limitations are:
- NVivo cannot merge two documents by any other means than copying/cutting and pasting text.
- It is difficult to format an image (change size, orientation, move).
- It is difficult to format a table.
- It is difficult to format a paragraph (hanging indent, first line different, line spacing).
- Copying from Word NVivo loses some paragraph formatting.
- Footnotes and endnotes in a Word document are lost after importing to NVivo. Word footnotes can however be manually replaced by NVivo Annotations (see page 91).
- Headers and footers are lost after import to NVivo.
- Page numbers are lost after import to NVivo but may be replaced by Insert page field in Word.
- Bookmarks and Comments are lost after import to NVivo.
- Field codes do not exist in NVivo and these are converted to text after importing to NVivo.
- NVivo cannot apply several columns, except when used in a table. When a multi-column document is imported it is displayed on the screen as single column. The multi-column design is restored when such document is exported or printed.

Often it is preferable to create a document in Word and then import to NVivo. Simply because Word is a dedicated and advanced word processor.

Tip: Formatting your Word documents for NVivo:
1. Give your Word documents meaningful file-names. If you write an interview per document, it is advantageous if the file-name is the name of the interviewee (typically using a pseudonym). After importing to NVivo, both the Source Item and the Case Node will be given this name. Put all interviews of same kind in the same folder, and consider the sort order. If you are using numbers in the file names then you should apply a similar series of names, with the same number of characters, like 001, 002, .. 011, 012, .. 101, 102, etc.
2. Use Word's paragraph styles to enable future autocoding. For structured interviews you should create document templates with subject headings and paragraph styles.
3. Whenever needed you can use Find and Replace and create headings with appropriate paragraph styles.
4. Divide the text into logical, appropriate paragraphs using the hard carriage return (ENTER on your keyboard). This facilitates the coding that can take place based on a keyword and the command 'Spread Coding to Surrounding Paragraph'. Remember triple-clicking!

6. HANDLING PDF SOURCES

Of particular interest to researchers who are conducting literature reviews, PDF documents will retain the original layout after import to NVivo and appear exactly as they were opened in Acrobat Reader. These PDFs can be coded, linked and searched as any other Source Item. One limitation is that PDF text cannot be edited nor can hyperlinks be created. Hyperlinks made in the original PDF, however, will function normally in NVivo.

Apart from bibliographic data with PDF articles downloaded from EndNote, new to NVivo, web pages can now be imported into NVivo as PDF sources. This new feature allows web pages to be organized, coded and queried the same as any imported .PDF file (See Chapters 15 and 17).

Importing PDF Files

1. Go to **Data | Import | PDFs**
   Default folder is **Internals**.
   Go to 4.

alternatively

1. Under **SOURCES** open **Internals** or any of its subfolders.
2. Go to **Data | Import | PDFs**
   Go to 4.

alternatively

2. Click on any empty space in the List View.
3. Right-click and select **Import → PDFs...**
   Go to 4.

alternatively

3. Drag and drop your file's icon from an outside folder into the List View.
   Go to 4.

In each case, the following dialog box appears:

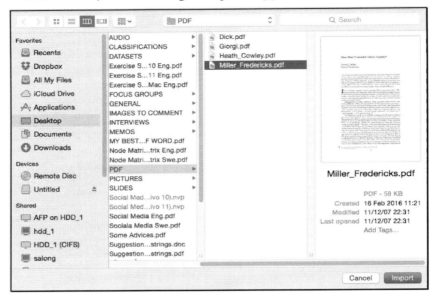

4   This dialog gives you all options to navigate your computer and select the PDF or PDFs that you want to import. Finally confirm with [**Import**].

> **Sticky Notes**
> in PDFs are very useful. You can create those with Acrobat Pro but also with recent versions of EndNote. Unfortunately NVivo cannot open these Notes. NVivo applies instead its link-tools, as a standard for all types of source items. Annotations serve the same purpose as the Sticky Notes.

When only *one* PDF has been selected the **PDF Properties** dialog box appears:

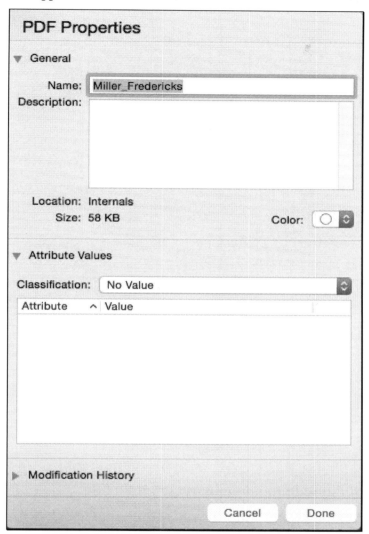

This dialog box will make it possible to modify the name of the PDF item and optionally add a description.

5   Confirm with [**Done**].

Here is a typical List View of some PDF items:

Name	Nodes	Refere...	Created On	Created By
Dick	0	0	Today, 14:06	BME
Giorgi	0	0	Today, 14:06	BME
Heath_Cowley	0	0	Yesterday, 10:58	BME
Miller_Fredericks	0	0	Today, 14:06	BME

Opening a PDF Item

1. Under **SOURCES** open **Internals** or any of its subfolders.
2. Select the PDF that you want to open.
3. Go to **Home | Item | Open**
   or right-click and select **Open.**
   or double-click on the PDF.

Please note, that you can only open one PDF at a time, but several PDFs can stay open simultaneously.

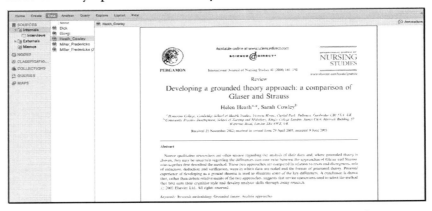

In this view you can code, link (Annotations, Memo links) and search and query as with any other Source Item. However, here is no option to edit a PDF item.

Exporting a PDF Item

Like most NVivo items, PDF sources can also be exported:

1. Under **SOURCES** open **Internals** or any of its subfolders.
2. Select the PDF or PDFs that you want to export.
3. Go to **Data | Export | Items**
   or right-click and select **Export...**

Exporting a PDF item can only be exported in the native PDF format.

> **Tip: Working with PDF text documents.** NVivo's functionality to work with PDF text documents can be a dream come true for researchers working on literature reviews. While many academic articles can be downloaded as functional PDF text documents, book chapters or other types of print material must often be scanned by researchers themselves. We recommend Adobe Acrobat Pro or ABBYY FineReader as software that will take scanned documents and recognize their text (a process called OCR, Optical Character Recognition).

> **Tip: Using Word documents instead of PDFs.** In our experience it is easier to work with Word files (.doc or .docx) than working with PDFs in NVivo. While it is not always possible to save your PDF files as Word documents, recent versions of Adobe Acrobat (X or XI) allow for PDF files to easily be saved as fully formatted Word files. Furthermore, Microsoft Word 2013 will allow for PDF files to be opened and saved as fully formatted Word files. *Also when you scan documents solely with the purpose of importing them to NVivo then create them as Word documents, which is the preferred file type.*

This dialog box appears:

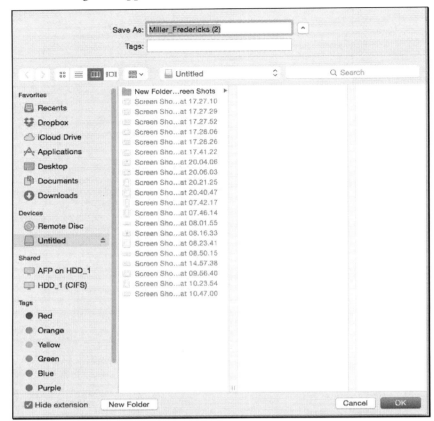

4   Decide file name and file location. Finally confirm with [**OK**].

Please note, that any coding made on such items cannot be transferred when the Source Item is exported.

7. HANDLING AUDIO- AND VIDEO-SOURCES

So far, we have mainly focused on text data, but NVivo has a variety of useful functions for researchers interested in working with audio and video data. NVivo provides two primary functions for handling audio and video source data. First, audio and video data can be imported into NVivo as a data source, which can be organized, coded and queried similar to text source data. But second, and perhaps more importantly for some researchers, NVivo contains a full functioning transcription utility for importing, creating, and exporting text transcripts. Instead of outsourcing transcription to third-party vendors or spending funds on specialized transcription software, NVivo gives researchers a very useful option for transcribing their own audio and video files within the software.

NVivo for Mac can import the following audio formats: .MP3, .M4A (as exported from QuickTime on a Mac) and WAV and the following video formats: .MOV, MP4, .MOV (as exported from QuickTime on a Mac). Several of these media formats are new to NVivo for Mac to allow users to import more media content form their smart phones. Media files less than 40 MB can be imported and embedded in you NVivo project.

Files larger than 40 MB must be stored as external files. Importantly, external files can be handled the same way as an audio or video embedded item. NVivo contains an on-board audio and video player for external files, so even though a large video file may not be embedded in your project, you can still view, transcribe, code, and query the file using the NVivo player. But remember, if you open your NVivo project on another computer the external file references will no longer work, unless you assemble copies of those files in identically named file folders on the new computer you are using.

Even the not embedded media items are located under the **Internals** or any of its subfolders as they are managed in all respects as if they were embedded.

The threshold value for audio and video files that can be stored as external files can be decided for all new projects with **NVivo → Preferences...**, select the **Audio/Video** tab, **Default for new projects** (see page 34). To adjust values for the current project, use **File → Project Properties...**, the **Audio/Video** tab (see page 42). To change for a specific Audio/Video item, go to **Audio/Video Properties** dialog box and modify Media Location (see page 67).

Importing Media Files

Importing media files follows a similar, simple protocol as importing text files or PDFs:

1. Go to **Data | Import | Audios/Videos**
   Default folder is **Internals**
   Go to 4.

alternatively

1. Under **SOURCES** open **Internals** or any of its subfolders.
2. Go to **Data | Import | Audios/Videos**
   Go to 4.

alternatively

2. Click on any empty space in the List View.
3. Right-click and select **Import → Audios.../ Videos...**
   Go to 4.

alternatively

3. Drag and drop your file's icon from an outside folder into the List View.
   Go to 4.

In each case, the following dialog box appears:

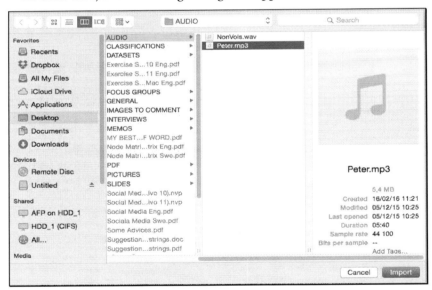

4. This dialog gives you all options to navigate your computer and select the media file or files that you want to import. Finally confirm with **[Import]**.

> Importing media files is sometimes not possible caused by the absence in your computer of an uptodate device called *Codec*. Often the problem is solved by upgrading with an appropriate Codec package. If so contact us for assistance.

When only *one* media file is imported the **Audio Properties/Video Properties** dialog box is shown:

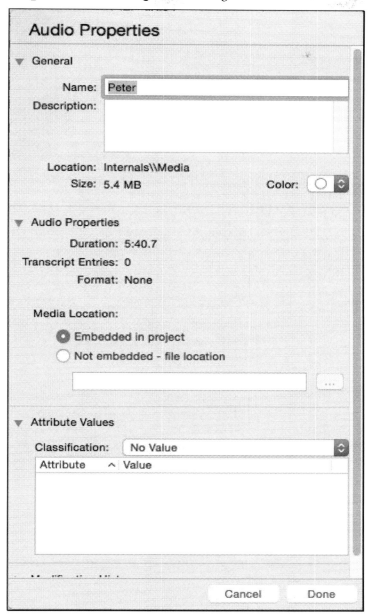

This dialog box will make it possible to modify the name of the item and optionally add a description.

Under Media Location you can let the audio or video file be stored as an external file even if the size is below the limit for embedding. After an audio- or video file has been imported you can change the properties from embedded item to external storage and vice versa by using **Audio Properties/Video Properties** dialog box. An embedded item cannot exceed 40 MB.

5   Confirm with [**Done**].

Here is a typical list view of some audio and video items:

Name	Nodes	Refere...	Created On	Created By
Cross Cultural Solutions...	0	0	15 Jun 2016 13:46	BME
JFK Man to the Moon	0	0	Today, 14:14	BME
NonVols	0	0	15 Jun 2016 13:48	BME
Peter	0	0	Yesterday, 20:26	BME

> **Tip:** We recommend hiding the waveform to make it easier to view a selection and other markings along the timeline. Right-click in the audio window and deselect **Show Waveform**, which is a toggling function. Each media item retains its individual setting during the ongoing session.

Creating a New Media Item

Instead of importing an audio or video item, a new media item can also be created:

1   Go to **Create | Sources | Audio/Video**.
    Default folder is **Internals**.
    Go to 4.

alternatively

1   Open **Internals** or any of its subfolders.
2   Go to **Create | Sources | Audio/Video**.
    Go to 4.

alternatively

2   Click on any empty space in the List View.
3   Right-click and select **New Internal → Audio.../Video...**
    Go to 4.

The **Audio/Video Properties** dialog box appears:

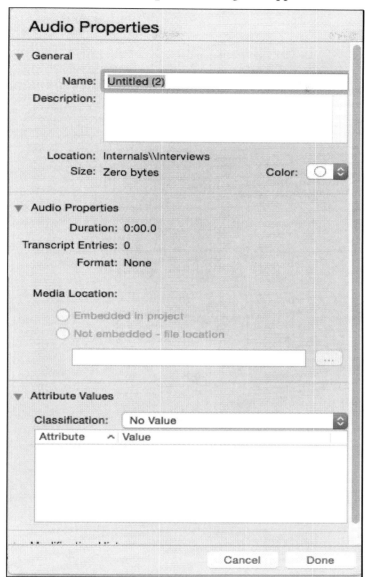

4   Type name (compulsory) and a description (optional), then [**Done**].

When you create a new media item it initially has no media file or transcript. Instead these pieces of information are meant to be imported separately. From the open media item, check **Edit** mode and go to **Data | Import | Transcript Rows** (see page 73). Importing media content in this case is not available in the current version of NVivo for Mac.

Opening a Media Item

1. Under **SOURCES** open **Internals** or any of its subfolders.
2. Select the media item that you want to open.
3. Go to **Home | Item | Open**
   or right-click and select **Open**
   or double-click on the media item.

Please note, NVivo only allows you to open one media item at a time, but several items can stay open simultaneously.

An open audio item with transcript rows, showing the waveform, may look like this:

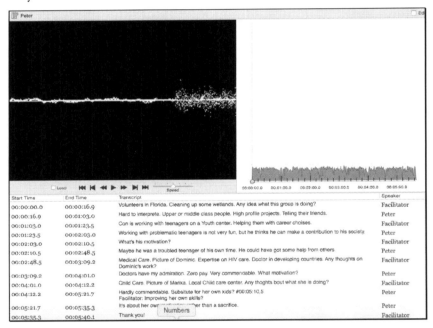

Provided a soundcard and speakers are connected to the computer you can now play and analyze the audio item.

Transcript Fields in a Media Item

NVivo for Mac has the following transcript fields as column heads for the transcript rows:
- Start Time
- End Time
- Transcript
- Speaker

Playing Media Items

An open media item has the following Play Control Panel:

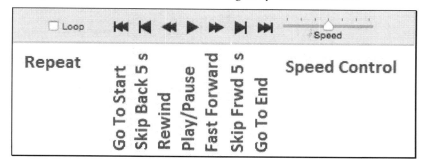

These commands are also available as right-click menus in the audio window.

The *Skip* interval is by default 5 s, but can be modified under **NVivo → Preferences**, the **Audio/Video** tab (see page 34).

Some key commands are also an alternative:

Skip Back is [**F7**]

Play/Pause is [**F8**]

Skip Forward is [**F9**].

Playback Speed

1. Use the Speed Control of the Play Contol Panel.

Selecting a Time Interval while Playing

NVivo acts like a simple audio file player. There are *two ways* to select a time interval that *can be used for* coding or for creating a transcription row.

1. Play the media item, possibly at low speed, using the Speed Control.
2. Determine the start of an interval by right-clicking in the audio window and select **Start Selection**.
3. Determine the end of an interval by right-clicking in the audio window and select **Finish Selection**.

alternatively

1. Use the left mouse button to define the start of an interval, then hold the button, drag along the timeline, and release the button at the end of the interval.

The result is a selection (a grayed section) along the timeline. Now you can code or link from this selection. The current selection will limit the play interval.

From a selection we want to add a new transcript row with a matching time slot. Click ⊞ or place the cursor in the transcript area, right-click and select **Insert Row** or [**Shift**] + [**⌘**] + [**I**].

A bit more complicated however industrious is transcribing while listening and using the toolbar in the lower part of the transcript area:

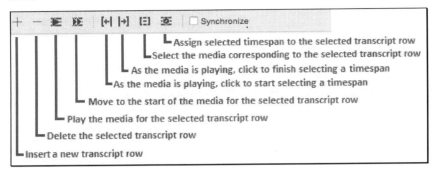

We start with listening to the audio file.
1. Insert a new transcript row with ⊞ or **Insert Row** or [**Shift**] + [⌘] + [**I**].
2. Start playing using ▶. You can pause, rewind, skip back and play again and start typing in Transcript column of the transcript row.
3. When you want to start a selection on the timeline click [←].
4. When you want to finish the selection on the timeline click [→]. Now a selection of a timespan is finished.
5. For assigning the transcript row start and end times click ▣ or [**Shift**] + [⌘] + [7].

Should you need to play the media item and comfortably read the transcript rows, scrolled and highlighted, check **Synchronize** above.

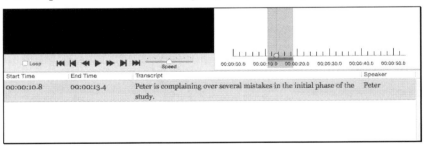

Should you need to adjust a timespan you can do as follows:
1. Select a transcript row by clicking in the row. The corresponding timespan along the timeline is then marked with a blue guiding line.
2. Make a new modified selection along the timeline.
3. Right-click in the transcript row and select **Assign Timespan to Rows** or click ▣.

As an alternative you can also modify the timespan directly in the transcript row by typing a new start time and a new end time. From there you can then make a new selection along the timeline.

1. Select a transcript row by clicking in the row item number (the leftmost column).
2. Click 🔲

alternatively

2. Play by right-clicking the Transcript row and select **Play Transcript Media** and the selection will correspond to the transcript row during playback.

Work Flow - Handling (transcribing while listening) media files

This is a summary in the form of a step-by-step procedure as applied when transcribing while listening:

1. Import an audio/video item.
2. Open this item in *Edit* mode.
3. Insert a transrcipt row with 🔲 or [**Shift**] + [**⌘**] + [**I**] or point at the transcript area, right-click and select **Insert Row**.
4. Start selection with 🔲 or point at the audio area, right-click and select **Start Selection**.
5. Start play with [controls] using pause, play, skip back, skip forward. At any time you enter text in the Transcript column.
6. Pause and finish selection with 🔲 or point at the audio area, right-click and select **Finish Selection**.

Work Flow - Coding Transcript Rows

1. Open the audio/video item in *non-Edit* mode.
2. Select text (certain words or all words).
3. Use the available coding options.

Work Flow - Analysing a node that codes an audio/video item

1. Open a node that codes an audio/video item.

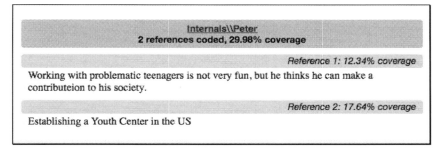

2   Then click on the top link **Internals\\Peter**.

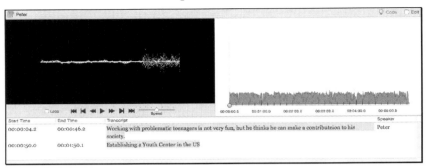

You can now read the whole audio/video item and the coded text is highlighted in yellow.

3   When you want to play an interval corresponding to a certain transcript row place the cursor in the transcript row, right-click and select **Play Transcript Media**.

> In our view even if it is possible to code a timeslot along the timeline the benefits in doing so is negligable. Coding transcript rows is the true and rewarding method. Playing a coded transcript row is easy with **Play Transcript Media**.

Importing Transcripts

In the event your transcripts are existing text files on your computer (perhaps you are fortunate enough to be using a transcription service for your project), it is possible to import text material as a transcript for its original audio file. NVivo allows you to correspond your transcript text with the audio file by using a structured text file format, .TXT, as follows.

```
Facilitator: Volunteers in Florida. Cleaning up
some wetlands. Any idea what this group is doing?
#00:00:16,9#
Peter: Hard to interprete. Upper or middle class
people. High profile projects. Telling their
friends. #00:01:03,0#
```

In this example `Facilitator:` will create the entry 'Faclitator' in the Speaker field, `Volunteers in Florida. Cleaning up some wetlands. Any idea what this group is doing? #` will create the entry 'Volunteers in Florida. Cleaning up some wetlands. Any idea what this group is doing?' in the Transcript field

74

and `00:00:16,9#` will create the entry '00:00:00.0' in he Start Time field and the entry '00:00:16.9' in the End Time field.

The importing of such text file takes place as follows:
1. Open the media item in edit mode.
2. Go to **Data | Import | Transcript Rows**.
3. Select the structured text-file with the transcript.

The following text box confirms the format:

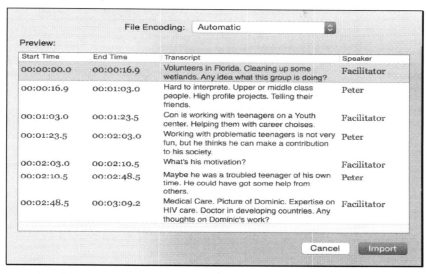

4. Click [**Import**] and the imported transcript rows are now included in the audio item and may look like this:

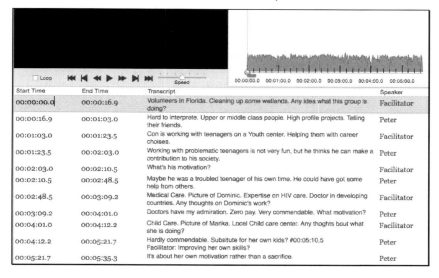

Linking from a Media Item

An audio item can be linked (Memo Links) in the same manner as any other NVivo item. However, hyperlinks cannot be created from an audio item.

1. Select a media item.
2. Right-click and select **Memo Link → Link to New Memo...** or **Link to Existing Memo**.

A Memo Link is shown in the list view, see Chapter 9, Memos, Links, and Annotations.

Exporting a Media Item

Like any Source Item in NVivo, media items can be exported:

1. Under **SOURCES** open **Internals** or any of its subfolders.
2. Select the media item or items that you want to export.
3. Go to **Data | Export | Items**
   or right-click and select **Export...**

A dialog box appears and you can select the file location. The exported audio/video items will take on the same names and file type as the project items.

You can also export the transcript rows separately:

1. Under **SOURCES** open **Internals** or any of its subfolders.
2. Select the media item that you want to export.
3. Open the media item.
4. Place the cursor anywhere in the transcript rows.
5. Right-click and select **Export...**
6. If you want you can rename the exported file. Choose among the following file formats: .DOCX, .DOC, .PDF, .TXT or .ODT.
7. Finally select the file location and finish with [**Save**].

8. HANDLING PICTURE SOURCES

In the same way that NVivo associates media sources with timespans which correspond to text (e.g., transcript rows), handling pictures in NVivo is about defining a Region of the picture which then can be associated with a written note, called a Picture Log. Both a Region and a Picture Log can be coded and linked. NVivo for Mac can import the following picture formats: .GIF, .JPG, .JPEG, .TIF, .TIFF and .PNG.

Importing Picture Files

NVivo can easily import a number of the most common image types. Plenty of free online image converter websites exist in the event you find you possess an image file that is a different format than NVivo accepts:

1. Go to **Data | Import | Pictures**.
   Default folder is **Internals**.
   Go to 4.

alternatively

1. Under **SOURCES** open **Internals** or any of its subfolders.
2. Go to **DATA | Import | Pictures**.
   Go to 4.

alternatively

2. Click on any empty space in the List View.
3. Right-click and select **Import → Pictures...**
   Go to 4.

alternatively

3. Drag and drop your file's icons from an outside folder into the List View.
   Go to 4.

In each case the following dialog box appears:

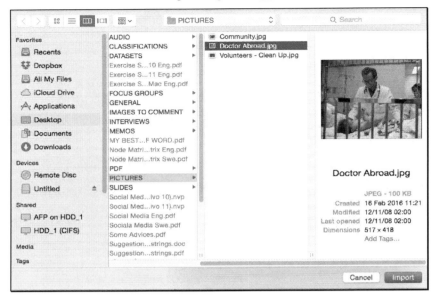

4   This dialog gives you all options to navigate your computer and select the picture file or files that you want to import. Finally confirm with [**Import**].

When only one picture file has been imported the **Picture Properties** dialog box appears:

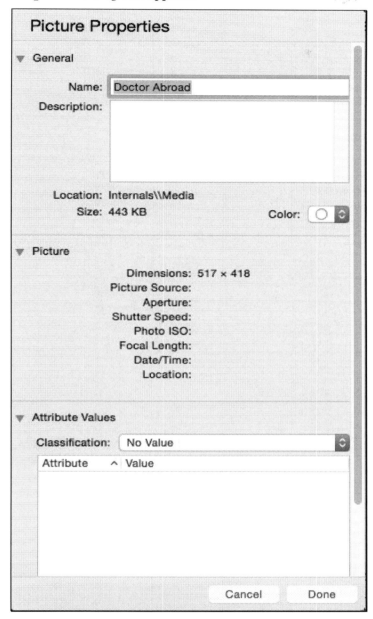

This dialog box makes it possible to modify the name of the item and optionally add a description. The **Picture** section gives access to details and data from the imported picture:

5   Confirm with [**Done**].

Here is a typical list view of some picture items:

Name	Nodes	Refere...	Created On	Created By
Community	0	0	Today, 13:55	BME
Doctor Abroad	0	0	Today, 13:54	BME
Volunteers - Clean Up	0	0	Today, 13:55	BME

Opening a Picture Item

1. Under **SOURCES** open **Internals** or any of its subfolders.
2. Select the picture item that you want to open.
3. Go to **Home | Item | Open**
   or right-click and select **Open**
   or double-click on the picture item.

Remember that NVivo can only open one picture item at a time, but several picture items can stay open simultaneously.

An open picture item can look like this:

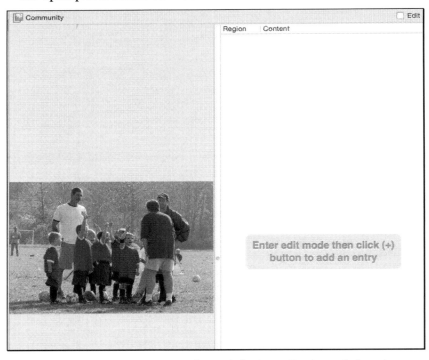

The handling of pictures is about defining a Region of the picture which then can be associated with a written note, a Picture Log. Both a Region and a Picture Log can be coded and linked.

Selecting a Region and Creating a Picture Log

1. When pointing at a picture the cursor turns into a cross and by dragging the mouse pointer to the opposite corner and release the button you create a region. To continue you need to allow editing; check **Edit**.
2. Right-click and select **Insert Row with Region**.

The result can appear like this and comments or any information can be typed in the cell below the column head Content:

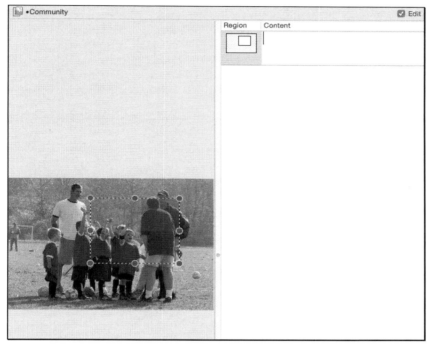

Sometimes you may need to redefine a Region and a Picture Log:
1. Select the row of the Picture Log that you wish to redefine. When selecting a Row the corresponding Region is highlighted.
2. Select a new Region (redefine a highlighted area).
3. Right-click and select **Assign Region to Row**.

In this way you adjust both a Region and a Row of the Picture Log.

Editing Pictures

NVivo offers some basic functions for easy editing of picture items. The following functions are found below the picture in an open oicture item:

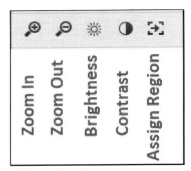

Most of them (not Zoom) are also found when right-clicking on a picture.

Linking from a Picture Item

A picture item can be linked (Memo Links) in the same manner as any other NVivo item. A Memo Link is not shown elsewhere than in the list view.
    1   Select or open a picture item.
    2   Right-click and select **Memo Link → Link to New Memo.../ Link to Existing Memo...**

When you choose an existing memo you will get a access to all not linked memos. When you choose a new memo you will name the new memo and you can create ite content directly.
See also Chapter 9, Memos, Links, and Annotations.

Exporting a Picture Item

This function is currently not introduced in NVivo for Mac.

9. MEMOS, LINKS, AND ANNOTATIONS

Memos, Memo Links, Hyperlinks and Annotations are NVivo tools that allow you to create connections and track your ideas across your data. While similar in function, each of these tools operates differently, with Memos and Memo Links being closely related.

Memos

Memos are a type of source that allows you to record research insights in a source document that can be linked to another item in your project. Any Source, Node or Case can have one Memo linked to it, called a Memo Link. For example, Memos can be notes, instructions or field notes that have been created outside NVivo. A linked memo cannot be linked to another item with a Memo Link nor can a linked item be linked to another memo.

A Memo can also be unlinked. Under **SOURCES** there is **Memos** folder (and possibly subfolders) where all Memos are located. An unlinked Memo is located in the **Memos** folder but not in the **Memo Links** folder.

Exploring Links in the List View

Memos, Memo Links and Annotations (but not Hyperlinks) can be opened and viewed in List View like any other Project Item. Under **COLLECTIONS** there are **Memo Links** folder and **Annotations** folder.

Right-clicking a **Memo Links** item in the List View opens a menu with the options: Open Linked Item, Open Linked Memo and Delete Memo Link. Exporting the whole list of items is also an option.

Right-clicking an **Annotation** item in the List View opens the menu with the options: Open Source and Delete. Exporting the whole list of items is also an option.

Importing a Memo

As with other Project Items you can import Memos or create them with NVivo. The following file formats can be imported as Memos: .DOC, .DOCX, .RTF, and .TXT.

    1   Go to **Data | Import | Memos**
         Default folder is **Memos**.
         Go to 4.

alternatively

    1   Under **SOURCES** open **Memos** or any of its subfolders.
    2   Go to **Data | Import | Memos**.
         Go to 4.

alternatively

    2   Click on any empty space in the List View.
    3   Right-click and select **Import Memos...**
         Go to 4.

alternatively

    3   Drag and drop your file's icon from an outside folder into the List View.
         Go to 4.

In each case, the following dialog box appears:

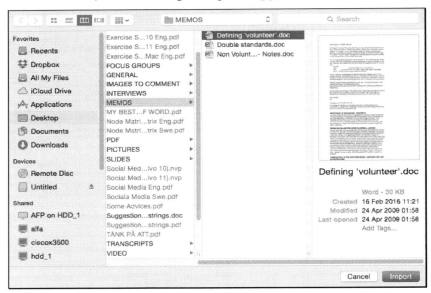

    4   This dialog gives you all options to navigate your computer and select the memo or memos that you want to import. Finally confirm with **[Import]**.

When only one memo has been imported, the **Memo Properties** daialog box appears:

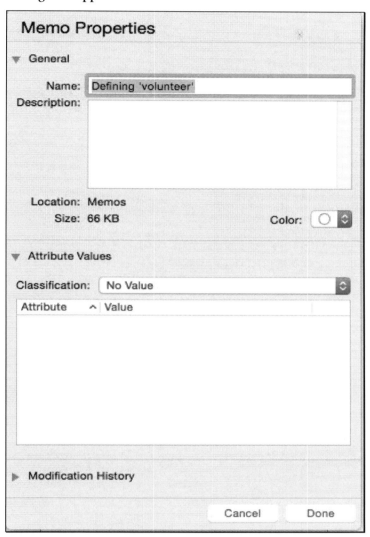

This dialog box will make it possible to modify the name of the item and optionally add a description.

5   Confirm with [**Done**].

Here is a typical list view of some memos:

Name	Nodes	Refere...	Created On	Created By
Defining 'volunteer'	0	0	Today, 20:22	BME
Double standards	0	0	Today, 20:28	BME
Memo som test för picture	0	0	Today, 16:07	BME
Non Volunteers - Notes	0	0	Today, 20:28	BME

Memos — **Linked Item**

In this example only one Memo is linked. The List View of Linked Items show the Linked Memos correpsondingly.

Creating a Memo
1. Go to **Create | Sources | Memo**.
   Default folder is **Memos**.
   Go to 4.

alternatively
1. Under **SOURCES** open **Memos** or any of its subfolders.
2. Go to **Create | Sources | Memo**.
   Go to 4.

alternatively
2. Click on any empty space in the List View.
3. Right-click and select **New Memo...**
   Go to 4.

The **Memo Properties** dialog box appears:

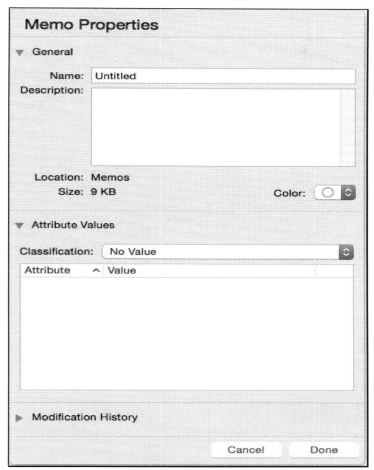

5 Type a name (compulsory) and a description (optional), then [Done].

Opening a Memo
1. Under **SOURCES** open **Memos** or any of its subfolders.
2. Select the memo that you want to open.
3. Go to **Home | Item | Open**
   or right-click and select **Open**
   or double-click on the memo.

Please note, NVivo only allows you to open one memo at a time, but several memos can stay open simultaneously.

Creating a Memo Link

Memo Links truly distinguish Memos from other types of NVivo sources. Memo Links are an optional component of Memos.

1. In the List View select the item from which you want to create a Memo Link. You cannot create a Memo Link to a memo that is already linked.
2. Go to **Analyze | Links | Memo Link → Link to Existing Memo...**
   or right-click and select **Memo Link → Link to Existing Memo...**

The following dialog box is shown. Only unlinked memos can be selected, linked memos are dimmed.

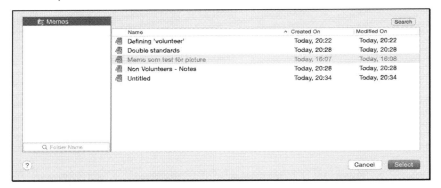

3. Select the memo that you want to link to and confirm with **[Select]**.

The Memo Link is shown in the List View with one icon for the memo and one icon for the linked item both in the foder of the memo and the folder of the linked item.

Creating a Memo Link and a New Memo Simultaneously

NVivo makes it easy to create a Memo Link and a new Memo simultaneously:

1. In the List View select the item from which you want to create a Memo Link and a new Memo.
2. Go to **Analyze | Links | Memo Link → Link to New Memo...**
   or right-click and select **Memo Link → Link to New Memo...**

The **Memo Properties** dialog box is shown and you continue according to page 87.

Opening a Linked Memo

A Memo can be opened as outlined above, but a linked Memo can also be opened in the event a Memo Link is in place.

1. In the List View select the item from which you want to open a Linked Memo.
2. Go to **Analyze | Links | Memo Link → Open Linked Memo** or right-click and select **Memo Link → Open Linked Memo**

Opening a Linked Item

A linked item can also be opened from a memo in the event a Memo Link is in place.

1. In the List View select a memo with a Linked item.
2. Go to **Analyze | Links | Memo Link → Open Linked Item** or right-click and select **Memo Link → Open Linked Item**

Deleting a Memo Link

1. In the List View select the item from which you want to delete a Memo Link.
2. Go to **Analyze | Links | Memo Link → Delete Memo Link** or right-click and select **Memo Link → Delete Memo Link**.

The **Delete Memo Link** dialog box appears:

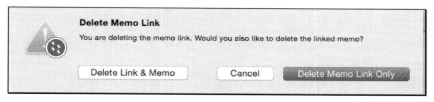

3. If you select *Delete Link & Memo* then also the Memo will be deleted, otherwise only the Memo Link will be deleted.

A Memo link can also be deleted from the **Memo Links** folder under **COLLECTIONS**:

1. In the List View select the item from which you want to delete a Memo Link.
2. Right-click and select **Delete Memo Link...** or use the [←] key.

The **Delete Memo Link** dialog box appears as above.

Exporting a Memo

As mentioned, you may wish at some point to export a Memo you wrote inside NVivo but now need to email to a collaborator.
1. Under **SOURCES** open **Memos** or any of its subfolders.
2. Select the memo or memos that you want to export.
3. Go to **Data | Export | Items**
   or right-click and select **Export...**

The following dialog box appears:

4. Decide file name, file location, and file type. (.DOCX, .DOC, .TXT or .ODT). Confirm with **[OK]**.

When more than one memo is exported the new files take on same memo names as they have in NVivo.

Remember, coding made on text items cannot be transferred when a Memo is exported.

Annotations

Annotations are similar but different. When you create an Annotation, the Annotation is available as an icon at the top bar of an open source item. An Annotation could be a quick note, a reference or an idea. Annotations can be applied to text items and PDF items. Unlike Memos, which can only link to entire sources, Annotations link to specific segments of your data (e.g., text from a focus group transcript). An Annotation in NVivo shares similarities with a footnote in Word, especially because annotations are numbered within each Project Item.

Creating an Annotation

1. Open a text item or a PDF item or a node coding such source items.
2. Select the text or other section area that you want to link to an Annotation.
3. Right-click and select **New Annotation** or [**Shift**] + [⌘] + [**A**].

A text box appears where you can type your Annotation. When you have finished typing, then click otside the text box which then will be hidden.

The Annotation links are colored blue and each Annotation will have a sequence number.

Viewing and Editing Annotations

When an NVivo item contains Annotations, you can open the Annotation link on the top bar of an open item:

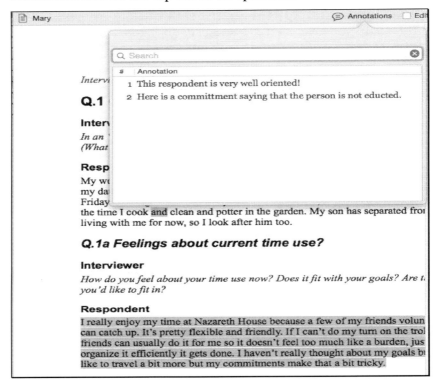

To close an Annotation window, just click outside the window. You can also point at an individual Annotation link and the following box appears:

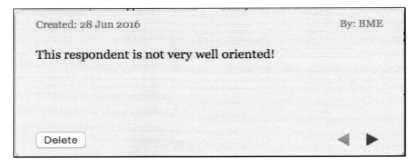

In this mode you can edit the Annotation or delete by clicking [**Delete**]. You can also browse to next Annotation with the arrows.

Each individual Annottaion is also in the List View under **COLLECTIONS** and **Annotations** folder. Each Annotation can be opened, deleted or when right-clicked you can select **Open Source**.

Hyperlinks

NVivo can create links to external sources in two ways:
- Hyperlinks from a text item.
- External items (see page 49).

Creating Hyperlinks

1. Select a section (text or image) in a Source Item while in Edit mode.
2. Go to **Analyze | Links | Hyperlink → New Hyperlink...** or right-click and select **Links → Hyperlink → New Hyperlink...**

The following dialog box appears:

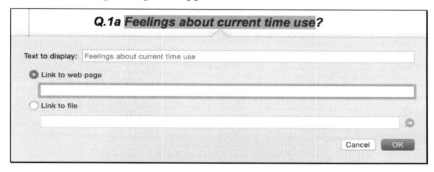

3. In 'Link to web page' paste a complete URL or in 'Link to file' browse with the [⊙]-button to find the target file in your computer or in your local network.
4. Confirm with [**OK**].

A Hyperlink is blue and underlined.

Opening a Hyperlink

The following three methods will open a Hyperlink:

1. Select part or the whole hyperlink.
2. Go to **Analyze | Links | Hyperlink → Open Hyperlink**.

alternatively

1. Point at the link and the pointer becomes an arrow.
2. Right-click and select **Links → Hyperlink → Open Hyperlink**.

alternatively

1. Point at the link and the pointer becomes an arrow.
2. Hold down the [⌘]-key.
3. Click on the link.

Editing a Hyperlink

The following two methods will aalow you to edit a Hyperlink:
1. Select part or the whole hyperlink while in Edit mode.
2. Go to **Analyze | Links | Hyperlink → Edit Hyperlink**.

alternatively
1. Point at the link while in Edit mode.
2. Right-click and select **Links → Hyperlink → Edit Hyperlink**.

The dialog box will allow you to edit and when done, click **[OK]**.

Deleting a Hyperlink
1. Select part or the whole hyperlink while in Edit mode.
2. Go to **Analyze | Links | Hyperlink → Delete Hyperlink**.

alternatively
1. Point at the link while in Edit mode.
2. Right-click and select **Links → Hyperlink → Delete Hyperlink**.

10. INTRODUCING NODES

By definition, a Node is a connecting point. In NVivo, Nodes are the primary tool for organizing and classifying source data. You can think of a Node as a 'container' of source material. Nodes can represent abstract concepts, such as topics, themes, and ideas. Nodes can also represent tangible concepts, such as people, places, and things. Remember, Nodes can represent anything you would find useful to organize and classify elements of your project. Some researchers know very early what kind of Nodes they will need to organize and categorize your data. You can create Nodes before you start to work with your source material. Other researchers may need to brainstorm organizational categories, concepts and structures 'on the fly' as they work through their source material. The way you work with Nodes varies largely depending on the methods used, the research situation and your personality.

Early on in any project, a good idea is to identify a few Nodes that you think will be useful. These early Nodes can be coded at as you work through your data for the first time. These early Nodes can be moved, merged, renamed, redefined or even deleted later on as your project develops.

NVivo also has developed a system for organizing and classifying both Source Items and Nodes, see Chapter 11, Classifications.

The terms Parent Node, Child Node and Aggregate are used when NVivo's Node system is described. A Parent Node is the next higher hierarchical Node in relation to its Child Nodes.

Aggregate[1] means that a certain Node in any hierarchical level accumulates the logical sum of all its nearest Child Nodes. Each Node can at any point of time activate or deactivate the function Aggregate and with immediate effect. The Aggregate control is in the **Node Properties** or **Case Properties** dialog boxes.

Theme Nodes and Case Nodes

In our work, we find it useful to make a distinction between Theme Nodes and Case Nodes. Theme Nodes are containers based on themes, your ideas and insights about your project. Case Nodes are containers based on cases, the tangible elements of your project, like your participants or research settings. Importantly, some nodes have the

---

[1] *Aggregate* has an imperfection in that the number of references is calculated as the arithmetic sum of the Child Nodes' references, which instead should be the logic sum as some references are overlapping.

ability to be labeled with customized meta-data called Case Classifications. A Case Node is understood as a member of a group of nodes which are classified with Attributes and Values reflecting demographic or descriptive data. Case Nodes can be people (Interviewees), places or any group of items with similar properties. A Theme Node therefore represents a theme or a topic common to the whole project. Theme Nodes are often represented by a Node hierarchy. The research design of many qualitative studies is often based on the intersection between Case Nodes and Theme Nodes. This is obvious for the design of Node Matrices (see page 142).

Interviews are often very important in a qualitative study. Therefore it is important ta have a basic understanding of how an interview preferably is represented in an NVivo project. It is easy to let the interview become a Source Item and the interview person becomes a Case Node. The document is the Source and the person is the Case. Demographic characteristics (e.g., gender, age, education etc.) are then applied to the Case the form of Attributes and Values. See Chapter 11, Classifications.

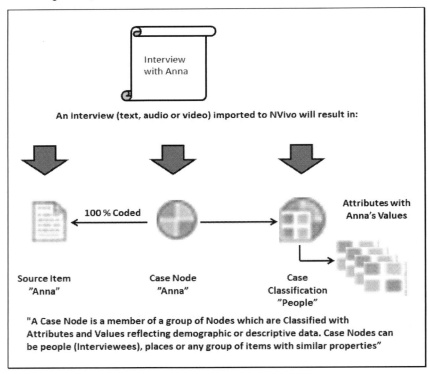

Creating a Node

Manually creating a new Node can be done in a number of ways.

    1   Go to **Create | Nodes | Node/Case**.
         Default folder is **Nodes/Cases**.
         Go to 4.

alternatively

    1   Under **NODES** open **Nodes/Cases** or any of its subfolders.
    2   Go to **Create | Nodes | Node/Case**.
         Go to 4.

alternatively

    2   Click on any empty space in the List View.
    3   Right-click and select **New Top Level Node.../New Top Level Case**.

The **Node Properties** dialog box appears:

> **Tip:** Some advice we offer coding newcomers is to record your thought processes in as much detail as possible when you are coding. The Description field of the **Node Properties** dialog box is an excellent place to capture why you have created that Node and how you think it relates to your coding hierarchy.

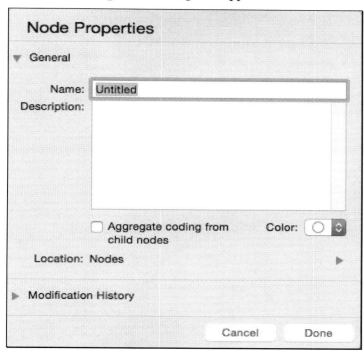

Alternatively **Case Properties** dialog box appears:

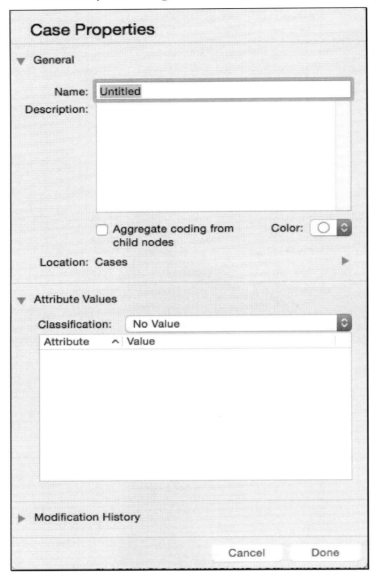

Please note that Cases allow for assigning a Classification whereas Nodes do not.

4 Type name (compulsory) and a description (optional), then [**Done**].

Here is a typical List View some Nodes:

Name	Sources	Refere...	Created On	Created By
Alfa	1	1	12 Jun 2016 09:22	BME
Beta	0	0	12 Jun 2016 16:08	BME
Coach	1	3	27 Jun 2016 15:59	BME
Key Terms	0	0	27 Jun 2016 08:50	BME
Misunderstanding	1	1	27 Jun 2016 16:04	BME
▼ Social skill	0	0	27 Jun 2016 09:13	BME
Many Friends	0	0	Today, 09:52	BME

And here is a typical List View of some Cases:

Name	Sources	Refere...	Created On	Created By
abba	1	1	12 Jun 2016 09:30	BME
Anna	1	1	Today, 10:04	BME
Bernadette	1	1	Today, 10:04	BME
Fredric	1	1	Today, 10:04	BME
Grace	1	1	Today, 10:04	BME
Ken	1	1	Today, 10:04	BME
Mary	1	1	Today, 10:04	BME
Nick	1	1	Today, 10:04	BME
Phoebe	1	1	Today, 10:04	BME
Sunil	1	1	Today, 10:04	BME
Untitled	0	0	Today, 09:53	BME

Building Hierarchical Nodes

As mentioned, Nodes (and also Cases) can be organized hierarchically. As a result there are Parent Nodes and Child Nodes in several levels of a coding hierarchy. Nodes can therefore form a sort of structured vocabulary, such as the MeSH (Medical Subject Headings) used by the Medline/PubMed article database.

Creating a Child Node

Assembling a Node hierarchy of Parent Nodes and Child Nodes is simple in NVivo:
    1   Under **NODES** open **Nodes** or any of its subfolders.
    2   Select the Node to which you want to create a Child Node.
    3   Go to **Create | Nodes | Node**
         or right-click and select **New Node...**
The **Node Properties** dialog box appears.
    4   Type a name (compulsory) and a description (optional), then [**Done**].

It is also possible to move Nodes within the List View, with drag-and-drop. When you drag a node on top of another node you create a child node. There is also an option to move a child node to become a top level node by selecting any child node, right-click and select **Move To Top Level** or alternatively drag and drop the node to its current folder.

Here is a typical List View some hierarchical Nodes:

Name	Sources	Refere...	Created On	Created By
Defining volunteer work	1	1	29 Nov 2015 15:15	BME
Family Values	12	77	16 Feb 2016 18:46	BME
▼ Reasons for Volunteering	12	279	29 Nov 2015 12:01	BME
Family Values	12	79	29 Nov 2015 10:08	BME
Motivation	12	103	29 Nov 2015 10:22	BME
Payments	12	42	29 Nov 2015 10:27	BME
Satisfaction	12	55	29 Nov 2015 10:30	BME

Underlying items in the list can be opened or closed by clicking the triangle, but also by selecting a node, right-click and select **Expand/Collapse Selected Node**. Using **Expand/Collapse All Nodes** all nodes in the current folder will be affected.

Merging Nodes

Any Node can be merged into an existing Node. Merging two Nodes simply combines the content of one Node into another.

1. Copy any node or nodes.
2. Select a target Node.
3. Go to **Home | Clipboard | Merge → Merge Into Selected Node...**
   or right-click and select **Merge Into Selected Node...**

Tip: If you select *Append linked memos* a new memo will be created with the same name as the new node. If all merged nodes have memos the new memo will append the contents from all its memos.

In each case this dialog box appears:

4. Select the applicable options, then click [**Merge**].

Alternatively, you can merge two (or more) nodes into a new node:
1. Copy two or more Nodes.
2. Select the folder under which you want to place the new Node.
3. Go to **Home | Clipboard | Merge → Merge Into New Node...**
or right-click and select **Merge Into New Node...**

alternatively
3. Select the parent node under which you want to place the new Node.
4. Go to **Home | Clipboard | Merge → Merge Into New Child Node**
or right-click and select **Merge Into New Child Node...**

In the dialog box select the applicable options then click [**Merge**] and in the next dialog type name (compulsary) and a description (optional). Finish with [**Done**].

Exporting a Node

All Project Items (except folders) can be exported in various file formats:
1. Select the node or nodes, case or cases that you want to export.
2. Go to **Data | Export | Items...**
or right-click and select **Export...**

The following dialog box appears:

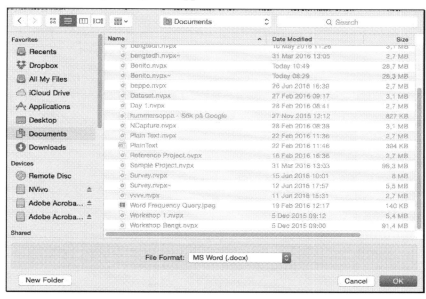

3. Decide file location, and file type. Possible file types are: .DOCX, .DOC, .TXT or .ODT. Confirm with [**OK**].

The Folder Structure for Nodes

The project folder structure emphazises on the important difference between Nodes (Theme Nodes) and Cases (Case Nodes). Node Matrices (see page 142) are also given a separate folder in the project folder stucture:

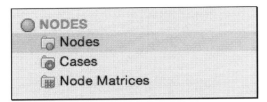

Under the heading **NODES** you will find **Nodes**, **Cases** and **Node Matrices** folders. These default folders and the names are not possible to delete, move or rename. However, the user can create subfolders to the **Nodes** and **Cases** folders.

11. CLASSIFICATIONS

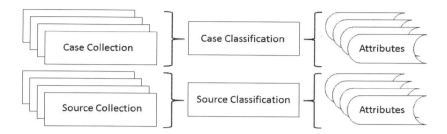

Case and Source Classifications

Nodes, Sources, Classifications and Attributes are related in the following way.

Sources (Source Items) hold primary or secondary data. They can be text sources, media sources or picture sources. Sources can be classified as described below.

Cases (Case Nodes) represent information that is generated from a certain source like an informant, a place, an organization or any other source that is subject to the current study. Cases can be classified as described below.

Nodes (Theme Nodes) represent a topic, a phenomenon, an idea, a value, an opinion, or any other abstraction or tangible object thought to be important for the current study. Theme nodes cannot to be classified.

Attributes represent characteristics or properties of a Source Item or a Case which has or will have an impact when analyzing data. Each such attribute has a set of **Values**. Attributes and values hold the demographic data of the study. For example, if gender is your attribute, the possible values are male or female.

Classifications are defined by NVivo as a collective name for a certain set of Attributes that will be assigned to certain set of Source Items or Cases. Classifications are not applied on Theme Nodes.

Classifications therefore fall into two types: Case Classifications and Source Classifications. We will explore how to create Classifications, how they are associated with Source Items and Cases and how individual values are handled. Attributes cannot be created without the existence of Classifications. This chapter presents examples of how to create a Case Classification, but the procedures are similar for Source Classifications.

Case Classifications

An example: You are part of a study looking at the experiences of pupils, teachers, politicians and schools. There are reasons to create individual Cases for each of these four groups:

- Attributes for pupils could then be: Age, gender, grade, number of siblings, social class.
- Attributes for teachers could then be: Age, gender, education, number of years as teacher, school subject.
- Attributes for politicians could then be: Age, gender, political preference, number of years as politician, other profile.
- Attributes for schools could then be: Size, age, size of the community, political majority.

Each of these four groups needs its own set of attributes, with each attribute requiring its own set of values. Each such set of attributes will collectively form a Case Classification.

Source Classifications

In NVivo, Classifications are also applied to Source Items with attributes and values. Source Classifications, for example, could be applied to certain interviews that may need attributes like the time of the inteview for longitudinal studies, place and other conditions. Source Classifications can also be applied to research that is the result of a literature review, with attributes like journal name, type of study, keywords, publication date, name of authors etc.

Creating a Case Classification

1. Go to **Create | Classifications | Case Classification**
   Default folder is **Case Classifications**.
   Go to 3.

alternatively

1. Under **CLASSIFICATIONS** open **Case Classifications** folder.
2. In the List View right-click and select **New Classification...**

The **Case Classification Properties** dialog box appears:

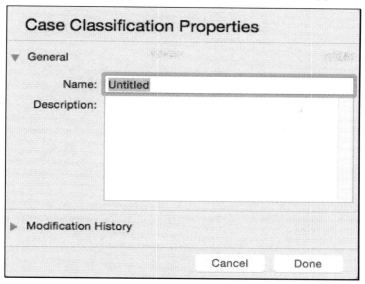

3   Type name (compulsory) and a description (optional), then [**Done**].

Creating a Source Classification

1   Go to **Create | Classifications | Source Classification**
    Default folder is **Source Classifications**.
    Go to 3.

alternatively

1   Under **CLASSIFICATIONS** open **Source Classifications** folder.
2   In the List View right-click and select **New Classification...**

The **Source Classification Properties** dialog box appears:

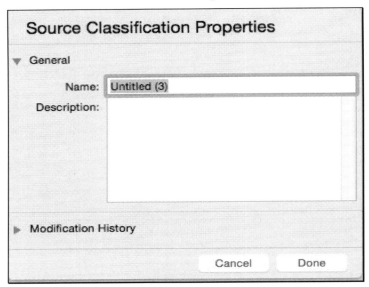

3   Type name (compulsory) and a description (optional), then [**Done**].

Customizing a Classification

A Classification can easily be edited. You can create new attributes and delete those not needed.

1   From the List View select a Classification.
2   Go to **Create | Classifications | Attribute**
    or right-click and select **New Attribute...**

The **Attribute Properties** dialog box appears:

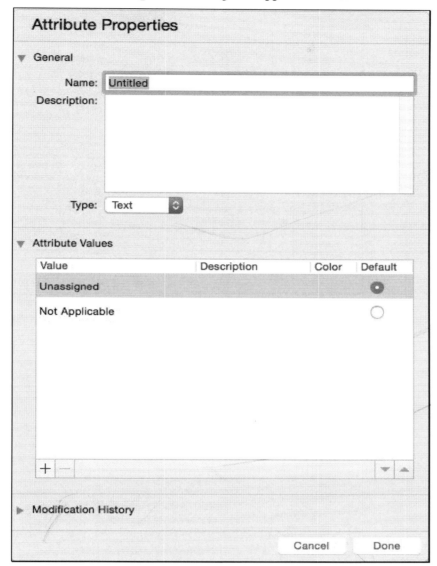

3   Type a name (compulsory) and a description (optional) and select the attribute type (Text, Integer, Decimal, Date, Date/Time, Time or Boolean). New values are created with the ⊞ button, then [**Done**].

The data type field indicates what kind of data will constitute an Attribute's Values. There are seven data types: **Text** data includes any text content (e.g., profession); **Integer** data includes a number without a decimal place; **Decimal** data includes a number with a decimal place; **Date** data is the calendar date; **Date/Time** data is a combination of the calendar date and time; **Time** data is the time in hours, minutes and seconds and **Boolean** data are binary pairs (e.g., yes or no, 0 or 1).

You can also decide which value is the default value. The default value is used when no other value has been decided.

Finally, you need to assign the Classification to a Case.
1. Select one or several Cases that shall be assigned a Classification.
2. Right-click and select **Classification** → <**Name of Classification**>.

Alternatively, if you only select *one* case:
1. Select the Node that shall be assigned a Classification.
2. Right-click and select **Get Info**.

The **Case Properties** dialog box appears:

3 Use the **Classification** drop-down list to assign any of the available Classifications.
4 Select the value for each attribute.
5 Confirm with [**Done**].

Working with the Classification Sheet

The overview of the attributes and values of Source Items or Cases is called a Classification Sheet. This sheet is a matrix where rows are Source Items or Cases and columns are Attributes. The cells contain the values.

While creating a Classification allows you to establish the Attributes and Values associated with classified items, the application of that metadata is done through the Classification Sheet. When a Classification Sheet is opened you can update values, along with sorting and filtering data.

This is an example of two Case Classifications with expanded Attributes in the List View:

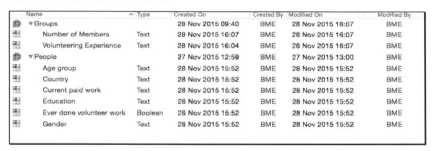

1 Go to **Explore | Classification Sheets | Case Classification Sheets → <Name of Classification>**.

alternatively

1 Select a Classification in the List View.
2 Right-click and select **Open Classification Sheet** or double-click on the classification.

Below is a sample Classification Sheet. As you can see, each row is an item that has been classified with the Classification Person, each column is an Attribute, and each cell contains the attribute's attendant value:

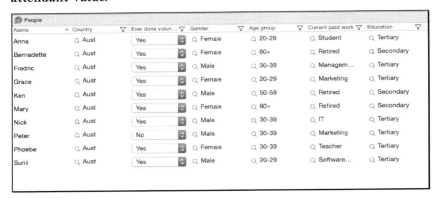

Once you have your Classification Sheet open, there are a number of options for structuring, viewing and occluding aspects of your data.

Hiding/Unhiding Rows and Filtering
1. Open a **Classification Sheet**.
2. Click the 'funnel' in any column head.

With this dialog box you can hide or show each column:

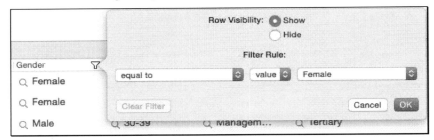

When a filter has been applied the "funnel" turns red. With one or more activated filters you can now go to **Layout | Sort & Filter | Filter → Filter Column** and modify the filter settings.

You can also got to Layout | Sort & Filter | Filter → Clear Filter on Column or Clear All Column Filters.

Sorting rows is made by clicking on a column head and one more click reverses the sorting order.

Resetting the Classification Sheet
1. Open a **Classification Sheet**.
2. Go to **Layout | Tools | Reset Settings**
   or right-click and select **Reset Settings**.

Importing a Classification Sheet

You can import a Classification Sheet as a tab separated text-file. All Cases/Sources (by name only), Attributes and Values are created from the imported file if they do not exist already.

1. Go to **Data | Import | Classification Sheets** or under **CLASSIFICATIONS** open **Nodes/ Cases** folder and click on any empty space in the List VIew, right-click and select **Import Classification Sheet...**

Tip: An easy way to convert an Excel worksheet to text is:
1. Select the whole worksheet
2. Copy
3. Open Notepad
4. Paste into Notepad
5. Save with a new name

The following dialog box appears:

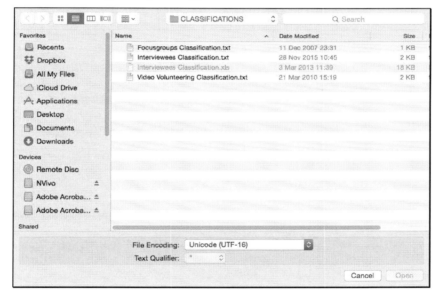

2. You can find the file that you want to import.
3. Click [**Open**].

The **Import Classification Sheets Assistant - Step 2** appears:

![Import Classification Sheets Assistant - Step 2 of 4 dialog showing: Specify how to classify sources or cases; Classification type: Case Classification; For text files: Create new classification "New Name" / Import to existing classification Groups; checkboxes for Create new attributes if they do not exist (checked), Update the classification of existing sources or cases, Replace attribute values of existing sources or cases that appear in this file; Cancel and Next buttons]

First be sure that you will import a Source or Case Classification. Next you decide if you want to create a new classification or use an existing one.

Create new attributes if they do not exist creates new attributes for the chosen classification.

Update the classification of existing sources or cases replaces the classification of the Source Items or Nodes that already exist in the location to be chosen.

Replace attribute values of existing sources or cases that appear in this file determines if imported values shall replace the existing ones.

4   Click [**Next**].

The **Import Classification Sheets Assistance - Step 3** appears:

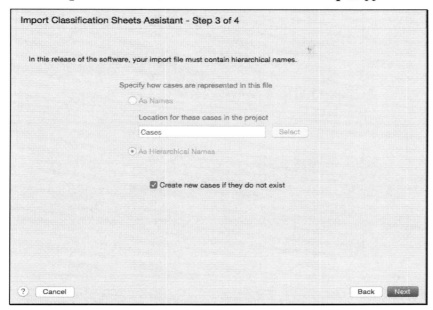

In this version of NVivo the imported file must contain hierarchical names.of the Cases (or Sources).

5   Click [**Next**].

The **Import Classification Sheets Assistance – Step 4** appears:

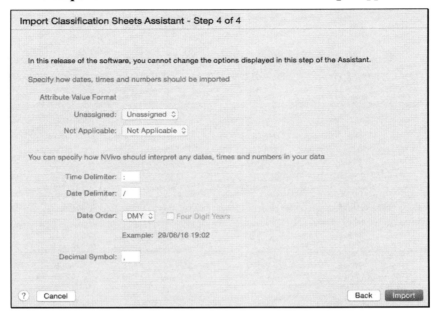

In this version of NVivo you cannot change the options displayed in this step of the Assistance.
    7   Import with [**Import**].
The result, a Classification Sheet in NVivo, looks like this:

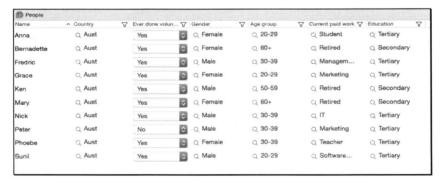

The Classification itself with its attributes can be displayed in the List View:

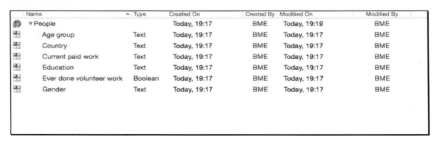

Exporting Classification Sheets

1. Select the Classification Sheet in Area 3 that you want to export.
2. Go to **Data | Export | Classfication Sheets...** or right-click and select **Export → Classification**

The following dialog box appears:

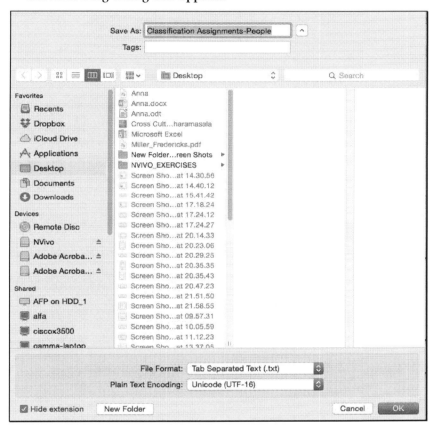

3. Decide file name, file location, and file type. Possible file types are: tab separated text-file or a comma separated CSV-file. Confirm with [**OK**].

12. CODING

Coding is the act of assigning a portion of your source material to one of your Nodes.

The item being coded can be any piece of data, even something as small as a single word from a document or single frame from a video. Nodes are the set of conceptual terms or case information that you will code at. One usually says that you are coding a certain source element at a certain Node.

As arguably the most important function of qualitative data analysis software, NVivo offers a variety of methods for coding data:
- Drag-and-drop
- Right-click/Menus
- Autocoding (only applied to Datasets)
- In Vivo coding
- Coding
- by Query

Here follows some basic definitions used both in the NVivo commands and in our instructions:

Code Sources implies that the entire content of a Source Item is coded.

Code Selection implies that a selected section in a Source Item is coded.

Code at Existing Nodes implies that a selection dialog box will appear for selection of one or several Nodes.

Code at New Node implies that the **New Node** dialog box will appear and you create and code at a new Node directly.

Code In Vivo implies that you instantly create a Node in the **Nodes** folder with the same name as the selected text data (max 256 characters).

The Coding Panel

NVivo for Mac includes a powerful tool that has been one of our favorites since it was recently released. The Coding Panel is here for Mac users, and it makes coding faster and easier than ever before.

To use the Coding Panel, open a source (or a node) and select a text segment that you want to code:

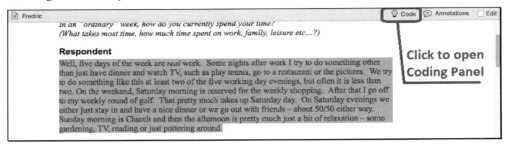

Next, click the Coding Panel lightbulb or use [**Shift**] + [⌘] + [7]:

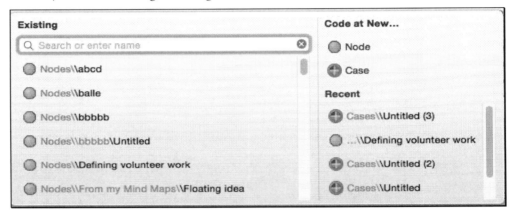

As you can see in the above diagram, the Coding Panel is split into two columns. Under the heading "Existing", the left-side column offers quick access to all existing nodes and cases in the project. A search bar allows you to simply type the code's name, or type out the first few letters and have suggestions appear.

Under the heading "Code at New...", the right-side column can be used to easily create new nodes or new cases. Simply, select [**Node**] or [**Case**] and a dialog box **Node Properties** or **Case Properties** will appear where you decide a name and location and possibly a description of the new item. Finish with [**Done**].

When you are in the midst of coding, the lower part of the right-side column "Recent" contains the most recent nodes or cases you have used. This allows you to quickly choose a code you are working with.

For now, the Code panel cannot be used for In Vivo Coding or Uncoding. We are hoping to see these features added to the NVivo for Mac Coding Panel soon.

Drag-and-Drop Coding

Drag-and-drop coding is probably the fastest and easiest coding method. Using this method and a customized screen is, according to us, the best way to code your data.

1. Under **SOURCES** open the folder or subfolder with the Source Item that you want to code.
2. In the List View open the Source Item that you want to code.
3. Select the text or image that you want to code.
4. Under **NODES** open the folder or subfolder with the Nodes that you want to code at.
5. With the left mouse button pressed, drag the selection from the Source Item to the Node that you want to code at.

When applying this method we recommend the vertical screen divider, see page 36.

Menus and Right-Click

While we prefer drag-and-drop coding, you will no doubt find yourselves in situations where you need to code using another method.

Coding a Source Item at a New or Existing Node

1. Under **Sources** open **Internals** or any of its subfolders.
2. In the List View select the Source Item or Items that you want to code.
3. Open **Analyze | Coding | Code Sources At**
   → **New Node** or
   → **Existing Nodes**

alternatively

3. Right-click and select
   Code Sources
   → **At Existing Nodes or Cases** or
   → **At New Node** or
   → **At New Case**

An alternative that will give you the same result (New Node) is when you select one or more sources, go to **Create | Items | Create As Node** or right-click and select **Create As → Create As Node**. The selected source items will be coded at one common new Node.

Coding Source Items at Cases

This function can be used when several Source Items need to be converted to Cases. For example, you can create a list of Cases if you have recently imported a number of interview transcripts. .

1. Under **SOURCES** open the folder or subfolder with the Source Item that you want to code.
2. In the List View select the Source Item or Items that you want to code.
3. Go to **Create | Items | Create As Cases** or right-click and select **Create As → Cases...**

The selected source or sources will be immediately coded at a new Case or Cases. One Case for each selected source will be created with the same name as the sources. The default folder is **Cases** under **NODES**.

Coding a Selection from a Source Item

While Case Nodes will often pertain to entire source files, though not always, Theme Nodes often involve selections from a Source Item:

1. Under **SOURCES** open the folder or subfolder with the Source Item that you want to code.
2. In the List View open the Source Item that you want to code.
3. Select the text or the section that you want to code.
4. Go to **Analyze | Coding | Code Selection At**
   → **New Node** or
   → **Existing Nodes**

alternatively

4. Right-click and select
   Code Selection
   → **At Existing Nodes or Cases...** or
   → **At New Node...** or
   → **At New Case...**

Uncoding a Source Item

As qualitative data coding is often an iterative process, sources may need to be uncoded.

1. Under **SOURCES** open the folder or subfolder with the Source Item that you want to uncode.
2. In the List View select the Source Item or items that you want to uncode.
3. Go to **Analyze | Uncoding | Uncode Sources At**
   → **Existing Nodes**

alternatively

3. Right-click and select **Uncode Sources → At Existing Nodes or Cases...**

From the dialog box with all nodes and cases you select the node or nodes you want to uncode at. It is possible to select all nodes and/or all cases.

> **Tip:** When you want to uncode a source item at all nodes (cleaning-up coding) select the source item, right-click and select **Uncode Sources At Existing Nodes** and select *All*. Only Node Matrices will retain its coding.

Uncoding a Selection from a Source Item

1. Under **SOURCES** open the folder or subfolder with the Source Item that you want to uncode.
2. In the List View select the Source Item that you want to uncode.
3. Open the Source Item that you want to uncode.
4. Select the text or the section that you want to uncode.
5. Go to **Analyze | Uncoding | Uncode Selection At → Existing Nodes**

alternatively

5. Right-click and select
   Uncode Selection → At Existing Nodes or Cases...

From the dialog box with all nodes and cases you select the node or nodes you want to uncode at. Only those nodes and cases that the current source is coded at are shown.

Coding and Uncoding an Open Node

An open node shows the coded segments of any coded source item. Therefore it is possible to both code and uncode an open node. The principles are the same as discribed above.

One specific function is available in this case, namely the command **Uncode Selection → At This Node**.

In Vivo Coding

In Vivo coding is an established term used within qualitative research long before dedicated software existed. In Vivo coding creates a new Node from the selection of text and then, using the *In Vivo* command, the selected text (max 256 characters) will become the Node name. The new Node's location is always in the **Nodes** folder. Node name and location can be changed later.

1. Under **SOURCES** open the folder or subfolder with the Source Item that you want to code In Vivo.
2. Select the text you want to code In NVivo.
3. Go to **Analyze | Coding | Code In Vivo** or right-click and select **Code In Vivo**.

Coding by Queries

Queries can be instructed to save the result. The saved result is a Node and is instantly created when the query is run, see Chapter 13, Queries.

Visualizing your Coding

Opening a Node
1. Under **NODES** open **Nodes** or **Cases** or any of its subfolders.
2. Select the Node or Case that you want to open.
3. Go to **Home | Open**
   or right-click and select **Open**
   or double-click the Node or the Case.

Each open Node or Case is displayed. If the Node has only been used to code text then the view mode tabs are: Summary and Reference.

The Reference view is the default, automatically selected each time a Node is opened:

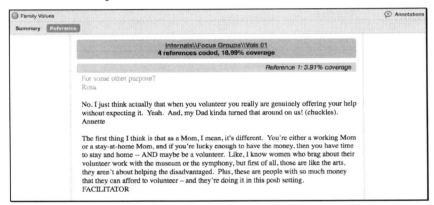

The text format displayed in a node is always *Plain Text* even if the source has other fonts, styles or attributes.

The link with the name of the Source Item opens the source item with the coding at the current Node is highlighted. Here the original text format is shown.

References coded is the number of coded segments (like a text-segment) of a source item.

Coverage means that the Node corresponds to a certain percentage of the whole Source Item that is coded measured in number of characters.

The Summary view is a list of shortcuts to all source items that are coded at the current node.

Viewing Coding Context
1. Open a Node.
2. Select the text or section that you want to show in its context.
3. Go to **View | Detail View | Node → Coding Context** or right-click and select **Coding Context**.
4. Select *None, Narrow, Broad, Custom...* or *Entire Source*.

The settings for Narrow and Broad are made in NVivo Preferences, section General, see page 32. By default Narrow is defined as 5 context words surrounding the coded segment and Broad is defined as Surrounded paragraph. The option Custom allows you to define the context setting.

Highlighting Coding
The coded text or section in any Project Item can be highlighted in brownish color. Settings made are individual to Project Items and are temporarily saved during a work session, but are reset to none when a project is closed.
1. Open a source item or a node or a case.
2. Go to **View | Coding | Highlight**.

There are several options:

None	Highlighting is off.
Coding for All Nodes	Highlights all Nodes that the Item is coded at.
Coding For Selected Items...	Opens Select Project Items showing current Nodes, other Nodes are dimmed.

Coding Stripes

The open document, memo, or Node can be made to show the current coding as colored vertical stripes in a separate right hand window. Coding stripes are shown in Read-Only mode or in Edit mode.

1. Open a source item or a node or a case.
2. Go to **View | Coding | Coding Stripes**

There are several options:

None	Coding Stripes are off.
Nodes Recently Coding	Shows the Nodes that are recently coded at.
Selected Items...	Is active when coding stripes have been selected.
All Nodes Coded	Shows all Nodes that the Item is coded at.
Nodes Most Coding	Shows the Nodes that are most coded at.
Nodes Least Coding	Shows the Nodes that are least coded at.
Coding Density Only	Shows only the Coding Density Bar and no Nodes.
Show Items Last Selected	Shows the Nodes that were last opened.
Number of Stripes...	Selects the number of stripes (7 – 200).

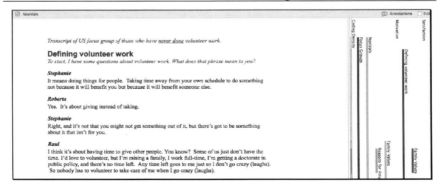

What can you do with Coding Stripes?

When you point and right-click at a certain coding stripe the following options will show: **Highlight Coding, Open Node..., Uncode.**

A click on the coding stripe highlights the coded area and double-click opens the Node.

By pointing at a coding stripe the Node name is shown. By pointing at the Coding Density Bar all Node names are shown that are coded at near the pointer.

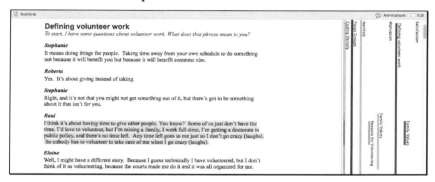

Color Marking of Coding Stripes

The colors of the coding stripes are automatically selected by NVivo. You can also use a custom color scheme, see page 24.
  1 Show coding stripes using any of the above options.
  2 Go to **View | Coding | Coding Stripes → Use Item Colors**.

Nodes without individual colors will be shown without any color. The default setting is **Use Default Colors** which are at random.

> **Tip:** Use limitation to **Selected Items** when studying **Coding Stripes** or **Highlight** for a source item. For example exclude Cases and study only Nodes, which means theme nodes.

Coding a PDF-Item

Coning a PDF-item follows the same principles as for other text-items. Opening a node that codes a PDF-item can look like this:

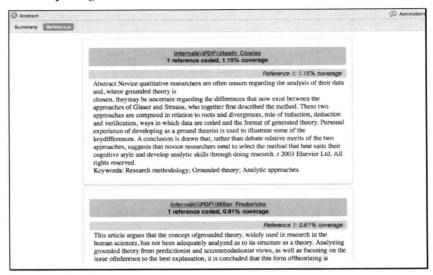

The text format displayed in a node that codes a PDF is always *Plain Text*. Clicking on the top link of the node leads us to the source (the PDF item) with the coded segment highlighted. In this case we have also activated the coding stripes.

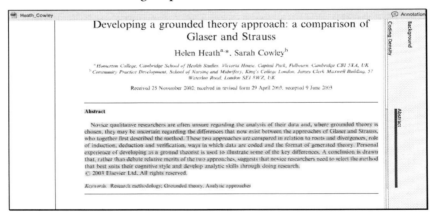

When you need to code a complete PDF document use any of the following commands '**Code Sources at <Node>**' or '**Create As Node**' or '**Create As Cases**'.

Coding a Media Item

With your newly created time intervals or transcript rows, you may want to begin coding data to correspond with project Nodes (Chapter 10, Introducing Nodes). Coding a media item can be done in two aspects of a media item::
1. Coding the transcript row or words in the transcript text
2. Coding a timeslot along the timeline

These two coding aspects are the same for media items as for any text material: select a text or a time slot to code and then select exsiting or new Node or Nodes, Case or Cases at which you will be coding.

If you want to code a whole transcript row, select all words ([⌘] + [A]), then right-click and select Code Selection at existing or new Node or Nodes, Case or Cases. Only remember in this case you need to be in a Read-Only mode (Non-Edit).

If you want to code a certain timeslot along the timeline, make a selection and then select existing or new Node or Nodes, Case or Cases, see Chapter 10, Introducing Nodes and Chapter 12, Coding. 1. In this case the chosen Edit mode (Non-Edit or Edit) is not critical

Showing Coding Stripes

Coding stripes is a useful feature related to coding text and coding of media items.

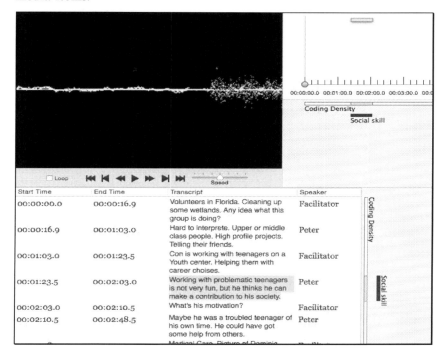

The screen shot above shows an example of a coded transcript row and a coded time slot. You activate the coding stripes by going to **View | Coding | Coding Stripes → All Nodes Coding**. The media item above is coded at the Node Social skill.

Clicking once on a coding stripe highlights in yellow the corresponding text or timeslot.

Double-clicking at a coding stripe opens the corresponding node.

These two options are also available when right-clicking at a coding stripe together with the option to **Uncode** at the current node.

Viewing a Node that codes a media item

When you open a Node that codes both a row and a timeslot it looks like this:

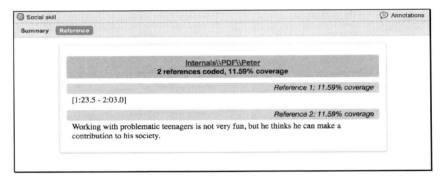

When you want to play a certain coded timeslot from an open node then you need to open the audio item from the top link above and select the transcript row (which is now highlighted), right-click and select **Play Transcript Media**.

Coding a Picture Item

You can code a Picture Log, a selected text element or a Region of a picture. The act of coding is in principle the same way you would code other elements of your NVivo project. In short you select data to be coded and then you select exiting or new Node or Nodes, Case or Cases that the data will be coded at, see Chapter 10, Introducing Nodes and Chapter 12, Coding.

If you want to code a row of the picture log, select all words ([⌘] + [A]), then right-click and select Code Selection at existing or new Node or Nodes, Case or Cases. Only remember in this case you need to be in a Read-Only mode (Non-Edit).

If you need to code a Region, select the Region with the mouse pointer and select a Node or Nodes, Case or Cases as usual. In this case the chosen Edit mode (Non-Edit or Edit) is not critical.

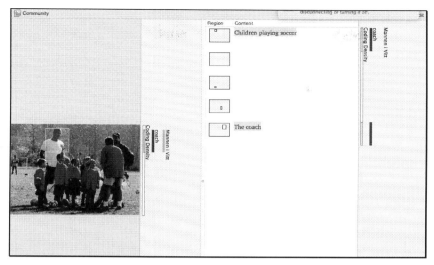

Coding stripes for a picture item are shown separately for coded Picture Logs and coded Regions.

The above example shows a picture item that has been coded at the nodes Coach and Mannen i Vitt.

We would also like to show when the node Coach has been opened. You will see both the coded region of the picture and the corresponding Picture Log.

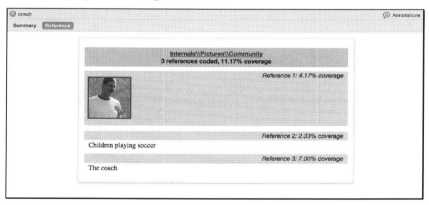

13. QUERIES

This chapter is about how to create and run various kinds of queries. In our experience, new NVivo users are sometimes intimidated by Queries – many types exist and using them effectively can take some practice. Remember, although not every query type will be right for project, every query type requires similar elements of foundational input. You will find queries increasingly simple once you read this chapter and learn the key features of a Query.

When you create a query, you first decide whether it will become a new NVivo item within the Queries folder (Area 1). The option button [**Save Query...**] is available in the dialog boxes **Unsaved Query**. This function lets you type a name of the query and optionally a description and it will be saved for future use. The saved queries respond the same as other NVivo items – they can be copied, pasted, and moved into folders. Query items open into query dialog boxes where you can adjust the settings of each query. Importantly, you will need to **Run** a query before you will see any search results; queries can be created without being **Run**.

You can construct simple queries that find certain items or text elements. You can also construct complex queries that combine Nodes and Cases with certain attribute values. The results of queries based on search words and Nodes and attribute values can generate new Nodes, sets or data visualizations like Word Clouds, or both. You can also merge query results with existing Nodes.

NVivo offers five different query types, Text Search Queries, Coding Queries, Matrix Coding Queries, Word Frequency Queries, and Coding Comparison Queries, which we discuss in Chapter 18, Collaborating with NVivo. Saving a query, editing a query, moving a query to another folder, deleting a query and previewing or saving results are dealt with in the next chapter, Common Query Features.

Word Frequency Queries

Word Frequency Queries makes it possible to make a list of the most frequent words in selected Source Items, Nodes etc.

    1   Go to **Query | Create | Word Frequency**.
       Default folder is **Queries**.
       Go to 4.

alternatively

    1   Under **QUERIES** open **Queries** or any of its subfolders.
    2   Go to **Query | Create | Word Frequency**.
       Go to 4.

alternatively

    2   Click at an empty space the List View.
    3   Right-click and select **New Query → Word Frequency**

The **Unsaved Query** dialog box appears:

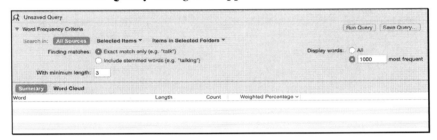

The options Exact match or Include stemmed words determine if qualified truncation will be applied or not.

    4   Default setting is *Search in All Sources* but the drop-down list *Selected Items* or *Items in Selected Folders* allow you to specify one or several project items.
    5   You can also set the minium number of characters and the maximum number of the most frequent words.
    6   With the button **[Save Query...]** you can save the query and the following dialog box appears:

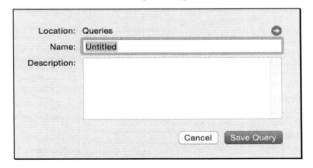

7   Type a name (compulsory) and a description (optionally) and use the [⊙]-button to decide the folder location of the saved query. Confirm with [**Save Query**].
8   Now run the query with [**Run Query**].

The Run command displays a Preview with two format options: Summary and Word Cloud. Word Frequency Queries cannot save the result and the [**Save Result**]-button does not exist here.

Summary View

Words in the Summary are sorted alphabetically and include stemmed words if the Word Frequency Query is set accordingly. Clicking the column heads re-sorts the list (toggling).

The Summary result looks like this, using the option Exact match:

Word	Length	Count	Weighted Percentage
theory	6	446	2,66%
grounded	8	348	2,07%
research	8	196	1,17%
data	4	147	0,88%
qualitative	11	123	0,73%
one	3	117	0,70%
glaser	6	109	0,65%
strauss	7	94	0,56%
analysis	8	84	0,50%
validity	8	70	0,42%
process	7	64	0,38%
may	3	59	0,35%
coding	6	55	0,33%
knowledge	9	55	0,33%
press	5	55	0,33%
categories	10	52	0,31%
discovery	9	51	0,30%
literature	10	49	0,29%

Using the option *Include stemmed words* it may look like this:

Word	Length	Count	Weighted Percentage	Similar Words
theory	6	470	2,80%	theories, theory
grounds	7	356	2,12%	ground, grounded, grounding, grounds
research	8	255	1,52%	research, researcher, researchers, research...
data	4	147	0,88%	data
qualitative	11	125	0,74%	qualitative, qualitatively
ones	4	120	0,72%	one, ones
glaser	6	109	0,65%	glaser
using	5	104	0,62%	use, used, useful, usefully, usefulness, uses...
validity	8	100	0,60%	valid, validate, validated, validates, validatin...
strauss	7	95	0,57%	strauss, strauss'
category	8	85	0,51%	categories, category
analysis	8	85	0,51%	analysis, analysis'
methods	7	83	0,49%	method, methods
process	7	81	0,48%	process, processes
issues	6	77	0,46%	issue, issues
coding	6	76	0,45%	code, coded, codes, coding
approach	8	74	0,44%	approach, approaches, approaching
tests	5	71	0,42%	test, tested, testing, tests

Select any one word (it is not possible to select more than one), right-click and the following options appear:

- *Export*, the optional file formats are: .DOCX, .DOC, .PDF, .TXT and .ODT). The complete list is exported.
- *Run Text Search Query*. The **Text Search Query** dialog box is shown with the selected word and its similar words copied to the search criteria and other options inherited from the current **Word Frequency Query**. The dialog box can be edited before you run it. See also page 134 on what you can do with Text Search Queries.
- Add to Stop Words List[2].

---

[2] Alternatively: Go to **Query | Actions | Add to Stop Words List**

Word Clouds

The *Word Cloud* view displays a word cloud based on your query:

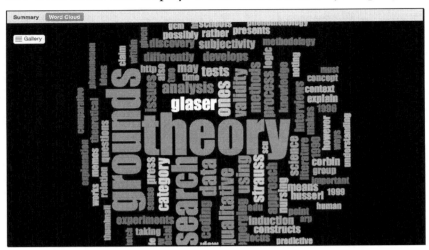

The Word Cloud displays up to 100 words. The size of the words reflects their frequency. Double-click on a word (or right-click and select **Run Text Search Query**) and a Text Search Query is created and runs with the selected word excluding its similar words copied to the search criteria and with results displayed as a Summary. Other modes available are: References (node preview) and Word Tree.

The button **[Gallery]** top left allows you to select various layout templates for your Word Cloud.

Text Search Queries

Text Search Queries search for certain words or phrases among items:

1. Go to **Query | Create | Text Search**
   Default folder is **Queries**.
   Go to 4.

alternatively

1. Under **QUERIES** open **Queries** or any of its subfolders.
2. Go to **Query | Create | Text Search**.
   Go to 4.

alternatively

2. Click on an empty space in the List View.
3. Right-click and select **New Query → Text Search**.

The **Unsaved Query** dialog box appears:

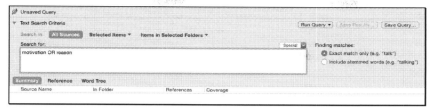

The options Exact match or Include stemmed words determine if qualified truncation will be applied or not.

4. Default setting is *Search in All Sources* but the drop-down list *Selected Items* or *Items in Selected Folders* allow you to specify one or several project items.
5. Type the search word or the search criteria in the **Search for** text box, for example 'motivation OR reason'.

When several words are typed in a sequence, e.g. ADAM EVE, the search is made as an OR-combination and when using double quotes, "GROUNDED THEORY", an exact phrase search is run.

All conventional operators can be applied in the search string plus a few more:

Option	Example	Comment
Wildcard ?	ADAM?	? represents *zero* or *one* arbitrary character
Wildcard *	EVA*	* represents *any number* of arbitrary characters
AND	ADAM AND EVA	Both words must be found
OR	ADAM OR EVA	Either word must be found
NOT	ADAM NOT EVA	Adam is found where Eva is not found
Required	+ADAM EVA	Adam is reqiuerd but Eva is also found
Prohibit	-EVA ADAM	Adam is found where Eva is not found
Fuzzy	ADAM~	Finds words of similar spelling
Near...	"ADAM EVA"~3	Adam and Eva are found within 3 words from each other

Operators **AND, OR** or **NOT** must be capitalized otherwise they will be interpreted as stopwords. Other search strings are case independent.

6. With the button [**Save Query...**] you can save the query and in the dialog box you type a name (compulsory] and a description (optionally) and the location of the saved query.
7. Run the query with [**Run Query**].

The Run command displays a Preview with three preview format options: Summary, References and Word Tree.

The *Summary* view (list of shortcuts):

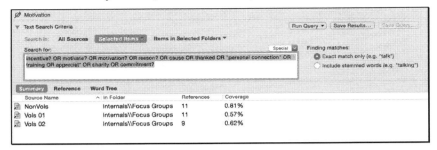

Double-click any of the shortcuts and you open the source item with the current search words highlighted.

The *Reference* view:

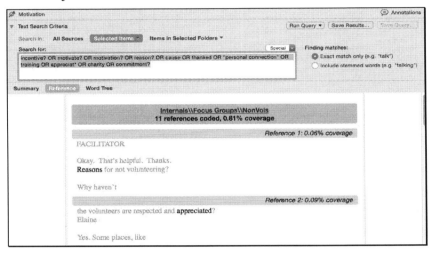

The *Word Tree* view:

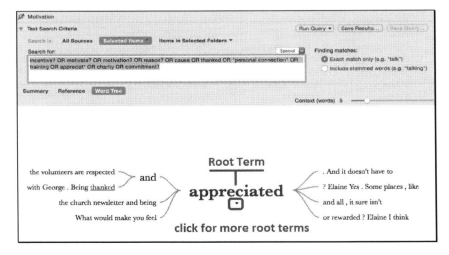

The Word Tree view is a feature for Text Search Queries that visualizes how a word occurs within a corpus of sentences. This is one of our favorite NVivo visualizations. Remember, to generate a Word Tree you need to ensure query options set for Preview which occurs before you save the result.

By just pointing at any branch of the Word Tree a "bubble" displaying the sources from where the branch origins.

Finally, you can also click any word of the Word Tree and the the whole branch will be highlighted. Clicking the Root Term will highlight all branches of the Word Tree. You can also select a branch, right-click and the following menu appears: Run Text Search Query, Export Word Tree.

In this case 'appreciated' is the most frequent Root Term. By clicking below the root term you will display a list of alternative root terms:

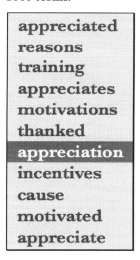

Each selected Root Term creates a new Word Tree. You can also decide the number of words (Content Words, default setting is 5) that surrounds a Root Term.

    8 When you are pleased with the result displayed in the preview you will now save the result as a new node. Click **[Save Results.]**.

The following dialog box appears:

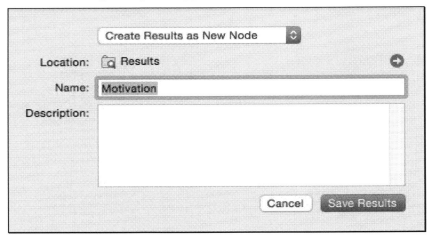

Create Result as New Node is default and cannot be changed.

9   Type a name (compulsory) and a description (optionally) with the [⊙]-button you decide the location of the new node. The options are the **Results** folder or **Nodes/Cases** or any of its subfolders. Once you click [**Save Results**] the new node is displayed and as for any node two format options are available: *Summary* and *References.*

The node which is a result of a Text Search Query codes only single words.

About Spread Coding

It often preferable to spread the coding so the context is more obvious. This action is called Spread Coding. There are several options for Spread Coding.

1   Open a node in Reference View.
2   Select the whole node, using [⌘] + [A].
3   Go to **Analyse | Coding | Spread Coding**
   → **Narrow Context** or
   → **Broad Context** or
   → **Custom...** or
   → **Entire Source**
   or right-click on the open node and select **Spread Coding** or
   → **Narrow** or
   → **Broad** or
   → **Custom...** or
   → **Entire**

There seems to be a refresh problem for large nodes (coding several source items) that can be overcome with the following procedure:

For any node wheather the node is a result of a Text Search Query or not (but not nodes located in the **Results** folder) then you click the [**Reference**] button.

Now you will see the result as single words beeing coded for all source items that you have chosen with the Query.

First you need to **scroll down** to the last reference.

Then apply Select All with [⌘] + [**A**].

Finally apply **Spread Coding: Broad**. The definition of Broad is set with Application Preferences, the General tab, see page 32. The NVivo default is 'Surrounding Paragraph' for text documents.

Should you apply Spread Coding a second time there is a risk of spreading the coding unintentionally to neighboring paragraphs.

Re-Running Saved Queries

A saved Query can be run anew at any time.

1   In List View select a Query.

2   Go to **Query | Actions | Run Query**

or right-click the query and select **Run Query...**

Each time a query is run the result is shown in a preview mode.

Editing a Saved Query

You can edit or copy a query at any time.

Changing the name:

1   In List View select a Query

2   Go to **Home | Item | Get Info**
    or right-click and select **Get Info**.

The **Text Search Query Properties** dialog box appears:

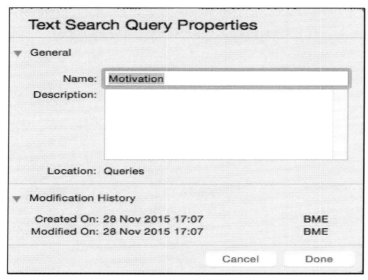

Here you can change the name and/or description. Confirm with [**Done**].

Changing the text search critera:
1   In List View select a Query.
2   Go to **Home | Item | Open**
    or right-click and select **Open**
    or double-click the Query.
3   Change any or all criteria and confirm wih [**Run Query**] and your changes will be saved. The result is a preview.
4   Finally click [**Save Results...**] and then you need again to decide location of the result. If you save the result with same name and location as an existing node, there will be a suffix (2, 3 etc.) added to the name.

Deleting a Saved Query
1   In List View select a Query.
2   Go to **Home | Editing | Delete**
    or right-click and select **Delete**
    or use the [⬅] key.
3   Confirm with [**Delete**].

Coding Queries

Coding Queries are advantageous when you have advanced your project's structure in such a way that you can acquire project insights via complex queries.

1   Go to **Query | Create | Coding**.
    Default folder is **Queries**.
    Go to 4.

alternatively

1   Under **QUERIES** open **Queries** or any of its subfolders.
2   Go to **Query | Create | Coding**.
    Go to 4.

alternatively

2   Click at an empty space in the List View.
3   Right-click and select **New Query → Coding**.

The **Unsaved Query** dialog box appears:

4   Each criteria row allows you to select Coded at *all of these nodes, any if these nodes* or *any case where*. For each criteria row you specify nodes or attribute values using the [🟢]-button.

To the right in the dialog box threre is an option to add or delete criteria rows:

An example of a Coding Query. Observe, the operators All and Any corresponds to the well-known OR and AND. The first line starting with **Search in:** sets the global limitation of the query. The option Selected Items can even limit the the query to certain Sets.

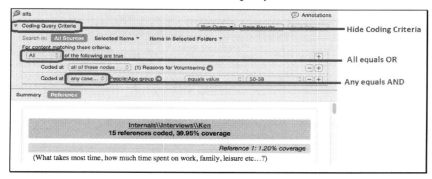

With the button [**Save Query...**] you can save the query and in the dialog box you type a name (compulsory] and a description (optionally) and the location of the saved query.

The [**Run Query**]-button runs the query as a preview and if the query is already saved modified criteria will be saved each time the query is run. An alternative is going to **Query | Actions | Run Query**.

The [**Save Results...**]-button displays a dialog box where you decide name and location (compulsory) and description (optional) of the node that is a result of the query. An alternative is going to **Query | Actions | Store Query Results...**

If you save the result with same name and location as an existing node, there will be a suffix (2, 3 etc.) added to the name.

The result of a Coding Query is based on existing nodes with most likely reasonable coding context why further spreading is normally not needed.

Re-Running, Editing and Deleting a Saved Query

Follow the principles described on pages 139 and 136.

Matrix Coding Queries

Matrix Coding Queries have been introduced to display how a set of Nodes relates to another set of Nodes. The results are presented in the form of a matrix or table.

Example: We want to explore how different age groups relate to certain selected themes represented by theme nodes.

    1   Go to **Query | Create | Matrix Coding**.
         Default folder is **Queries**.
         Go to 4.

alternatively

    1   Under **QUERIES** open **Queries** or any of its subfolders.
    2   Go to **Query | Create | Matrix Coding**.
         Go to 4.

alternatively

    2   Click at an empty space in the List View.
    3   Right-click and select **New Query → Matrix Coding**.

The **Unsaved Query** dialog box appears:

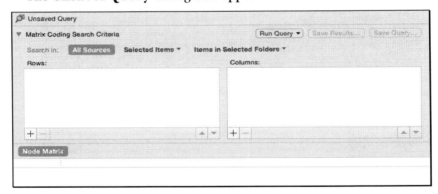

The first line starting with **Search in:** sets the global limitation of the query. The option Selected Items can even limit the the query to certain Sets.

    4   First specify Rows in the left text box.
         Clicking on the [+] gives you the options *Select Items...* or *Select Attribute Values...*
    5   Next specify Columns in the right text box.
         Clicking on the [+] gives you the options *Select Items...* or *Select Attribute Values...*
         Clicking on the [-] deletes the selected item(s) in the criterion.

When you have specified rows and columns according to the analytic study, the dialog box looks like this:

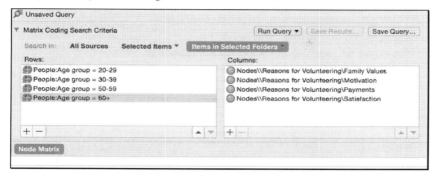

With the button [**Save Query...**] you can save the query and in the dialog box you type a name (compulsory] and a description (optionally) and the location of the saved query.

The [**Run Query**]-button runs the query as a preview and when the query is already saved modified criteria will be saved each time the query is run. An alternative is going to **Query | Actions | Run Query**.

The result preview is now displayed in the ower part of the **Unsaved Query** dialog box:

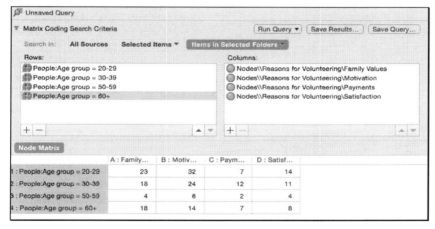

The [**Save Results...**]-button displays a dialog box where you decide name (compulsory), description (optional) and location of the result. The location options are the **Results** folder or the **Node Matrices** folder. An alternative is going to **Query | Actions | Store Query Results...**

If you save the result with same name and location as an existing node, there will be a suffix (2, 3 etc.) added to the name. Finally click [**Save Results**] in this dialog box.

Opening a Cell

A matrix is a collection of cells. Each cell is a Node. You may need therefore to study each cell separately.

1. Open the matrix.
2. Select the cell you want to open.
3. Right-click and select **Open Node Matrix Cell** or double-click the cell.

The cell opens and can be analyzed as any other node. This Node is an integral part of the matrix and if you want to save it as a new Node then select the whole Node (or part thereof if preferred) in the Reference view mode and go to **Analyze | Coding | Code Selection At → New Node** or right-click and select **Code Selection → At New Node...**

Viewing Cell Content

There are several options to view cell content when cells are not opened. The default view displays the number of coding references and presently other viewing options are not at hand. Various shading options can however be selected.

1. Open the matrix.
2. Go to **View | Detail View | Node Matrix →** <select> any of the following options:

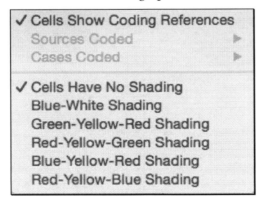

Re-Running, Editing and Deleting a Saved Query

Follow the principles described on pages 139 and 136.

14. COMMON QUERY FEATURES

This chapter deals with the functions and features common to several types of queries.

Saving a Query

As mentioned at the beginning of previous chapter, Queries made can be saved so that they can be run again at a later stage.

When you are creating a new query you will first reach the **Unsaved Query** dialog box. As soon as you have begun to type input data in the Search for text box the [**Save Query**]-button as activated and you can save the query with a name, description and a location.

Spread Coding

When you have run a Text Search Query the result is a node with single words from the input in the search string.

Usually any type of Spread Coding is preferred. The options are: Narrow, Broad, Custom... and Entire. Spread coding can only be applied when a node is open in Reference view. From there you select one or more references or the whole node, right-click and apply the mentioned options.

The definitions of Narrow and Broad are set in the NVivo Preferences, the General tab, see page 32.

Saving a Result

Applying Run Query from the **Unsaved Query** dialog box always displays the result as a preview and therefore not saved. As the next action you need to apply [**Save Results**]. The dialog box that follows offers options for the location of the new node: **Nodes, Cases** or **Node Matrices** any of its subfolders or the **Results** folder.

The result of a Word Frquency Query cannot be saved as mentioned earlier.

About the Results Folder

The Results folder is the default folder where a result of query is saved. You can however modify the settings so that query results will be saved in any Node location. But there are some advantages to using the **Results** folder.

First, it is practical to see if the result is reasonable (before it is saved in its final location or made into a Node) or if the query needs immediate modification.

Be aware that a preview can sometimes serve the same purpose.

Nodes in the Results folder cannot be edited or used for further coding or uncoding and commands like **Uncode At this Node** and **Spread Coding** are unavailable. After verifying your Node in the

Results folder you should move the result to a location under Nodes or Cases, where it can be more fully analyzed.

When you run a Text Search Query that is saved in the Results folder Coding Context Narrow (5 words) is activated, but the Coding Context is reset as soon as the Node is moved to a location under Nodes or Cases. If you then should need Coding Context this feature can be activated with a separate command (see page 123).

Editing a Query

A saved query can be edited or re-run anytime:
1. Under **QUERIES** open **Queries** or any of its subfolders.
2. Select the query in the List View that you want to edit.
3. Go to **Home | Item | Open**
   or right-click and select **Open**
   or double-click the query.

The dialog box for an idividual query appears. You may now make any modifications and as soon as you run the query your modifications are saved. Then you can carry on by saving the result.

Last Run Query Option

The last Query that has been used during the ongoing work session can comfortably be revoked by this command:
1. Go to **Query | Actions | Last Run Query**.

15. HANDLING BIBLIOGRAPHIC DATA

Along with source material that is gathered as project evidence, reference material (e.g., peer-reviewed academic research papers) often play a crucial role in grounding a qualitative research project. NVivo for Mac also allows users to import reference material, including full-text documents, from common reference handling software like EndNote, RefWorks, Zotero, and Mendelay. When imported, reference materials become Source Items and as a result they can be coded and analyzed the same way as other sources. For advanced analysis, we offer sverla options uing queries to efficiently work with academic reference material, such as Literature Reviews. This chapter is about importing bibliographic data stored in certain selected reference handling software. The file formats that can be imported to NVivo are: .XML for EndNote and .RIS for RefWorks, Zotero, and Mendelay.

In this chapter, we will use as an example importing data into NVivo from EndNote (the top reference handling software, in our opinion). The following two reference records will be exported from Endnote:

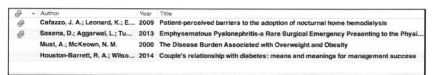

The clip symbol indicates that one reference has a file attachment (typically a PDF full text article) and the other not.

On the next page, you will see a shot of a typical reference from EndNote. As you can see, each reference listing contains a wealth of meta-data about a single reference:

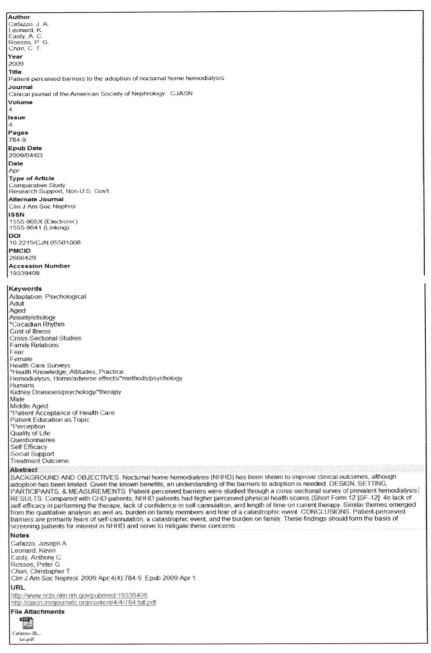

    The communication between reference handling software and NVivo is in the form of an XML structured file. Reference handling software typically allows you to export a collection of citations. The export command from for EndNote is **File → Export** and the file type must be set as XML. This creates you a file with all the above information including a file path to the PDF.

Importing Bibliographic Data

In NVivo go to **Data | Import | EndNote**. With the file browser you will find the XML-file you exported from your reference handling software. Click [**Open**].

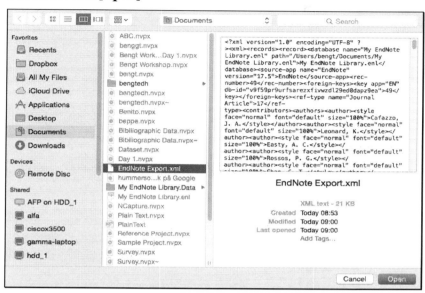

The **Import Bibliographic Data Assistant - Step 1** appears:

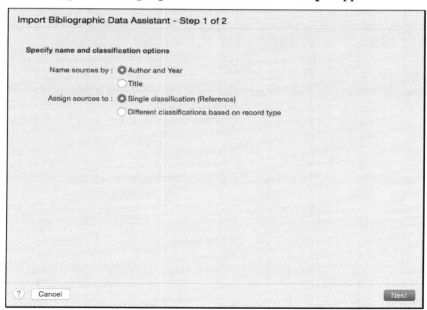

The first option is under **Name sources by** and the alternatives are: Author and Year or Title.

The second option is to decide if you want one Source Classification for all your bibliographic data, Reference. Then there will be one attribute called Reference Type and the values will be Journal Article, Book, Conference Proceedings etc. If this is your preference then select
Assign sources to: Single classification (Reference).
If you instead prefer one Source Classification for each reference type then select
Assign sources to: Different classifications based on record type.

If you want to import file attachments (PDFs or figures) then check Import source content from file attachments and if you want to create memos from abstract etc then check Create memos from abstract, keywords and notes.

When options are selected click [**Next**].
The **Import Bibliographic Data Assistant – Step 2** appears:

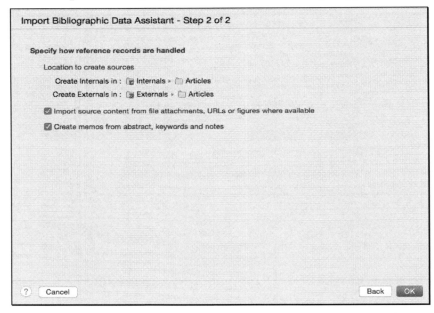

Here you decide the folder (**Internals** or any of its subfolder) where records with file attachments (PDFs or figures) are stored and the folder (**Externals** or any of its subfolder) where records without file attachments are stored.

When settings are done, click [**OK**].

The PDF Source Item

The internal PDF Source Item has the same look and layout as the original article and can now be coded, linked, searched and queried:

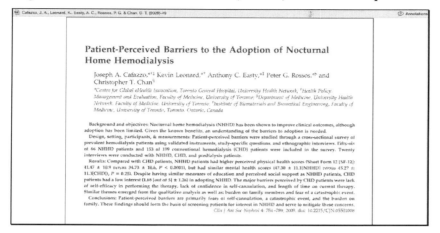

The **PDF Properties** dialog box (select the PDF item, right-click and select **Get Info**) has now the following content imported through the XML file. The name of the PDF-item is the name of the EndNote file attachment, which can be set in EndNote to correspond to the title of the article. As you can see below, the abstract has been copied into the Description field of the PDF source:

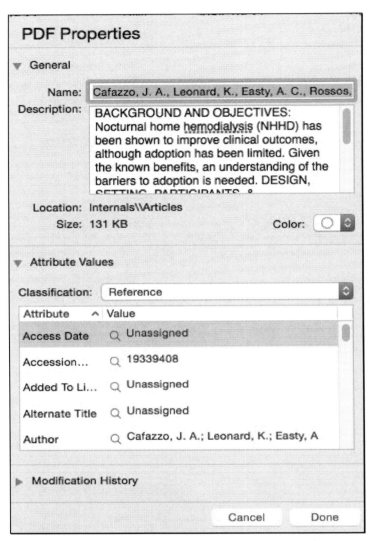

As you can see from the lower part of the dialog box a Source Classification called *Reference* has been created and the attibutes and values correspond to the field names and its content from EndNote. Close with [**Done**].

The Linked Memo

If you have chosen to create a linked memo it will have the same name as the linked item. The memo is a normal text document and can be edited and otherwise handled as any Source Item. The content in our example is from the Abstract, Keywords and Notes fields of the original reference record. This is a useful feature because it allows you to search and code the abstract, which is not possible when the abstract is only located in the Description field.

> Cafazzo, J. A., Leonard, K., Easty, A. C., Rossos, P. G. & Chan, C. T. (2009)-49 Imported Notes
>
> {Abstract}
> BACKGROUND AND OBJECTIVES: Nocturnal home hemodialysis (NHHD) has been shown to improve clinical outcomes, although adoption has been limited. Given the known benefits, an understanding of the barriers to adoption is needed. DESIGN, SETTING, PARTICIPANTS, & MEASUREMENTS: Patient-perceived barriers were studied through a cross-sectional survey of prevalent hemodialysis patients using validated instruments, study-specific questions, and ethnographic interviews. Fifty-six of 66 NHHD patients and 153 of 199 conventional hemodialysis (CHD) patients were included in the survey. Twenty interviews were conducted with NHHD, CHD, and predialysis patients. RESULTS: Compared with CHD patients, NHHD patients had higher perceived physical health scores (Short Form 12 [SF-12]: 41.47 +/- 10.9 versus 34.73 +/- 10.6, $P < 0.0001$), but had similar mental health scores (47.30 +/- 11.1[NHHD] versus 45.27 +/- 11.3[CHD], $P = 0.25$). Despite having similar measures of education and perceived social support as NHHD patients, CHD patients had a low interest (1.68 [out of 5] +/- 1.26) in adopting NHHD. The major barriers perceived by CHD patients were lack of self-efficacy in performing the therapy, lack of confidence in self-cannulation, and length of time on current therapy. Similar themes emerged from the qualitative analysis as well as: burden on family members and fear of a catastrophic event. CONCLUSIONS: Patient-perceived barriers are primarily fears of self-cannulation, a catastrophic event, and the burden on family. These findings should form the basis of screening patients for interest in NHHD and serve to mitigate these concerns.
>
> {Keywords}
> Adaptation, Psychological; Adult; Aged; Anxiety/etiology; *Circadian Rhythm; Cost of Illness; Cross-Sectional Studies; Family Relations; Fear; Female; Health Care Surveys; *Health Knowledge, Attitudes, Practice; Hemodialysis, Home/adverse effects/*methods/psychology; Humans; Kidney Diseases/psychology/*therapy; Male; Middle Aged; *Patient Acceptance of Health Care; Patient Education as Topic; *Perception; Quality of Life; Self Efficacy; Social Support; Surveys and Questionnaires; Treatment Outcome
>
> {Notes}
> Cafazzo, Joseph A Leonard, Kevin Easty, Anthony C Rossos, Peter G Chan, Christopher T eng Comparative Study Research Support, Non-U.S. Gov't 2009/04/03 09:00 Clin J Am Soc Nephrol. 2009 Apr;4(4):784-9. doi: 10.2215/CJN.05501008. Epub 2009 Apr 1.

The **Memo Properties** (select the memo, right-click and select **Get Info**) has now the following content:

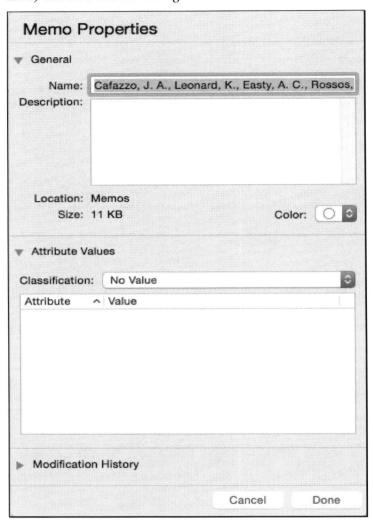

Please note, that the memos are not classified nor do they have any description filled in by default. Close with [**Done**].

The External Source Item

Bibiographic records without file attachments (like PDFs) are imported as External source items. These items have usually a link leading to the external source from where the records were captured. External items have also a linked Memo with similar properties as explained above. Exploring the External Properties you will find that the description field has a copy of the abstract like the Internals have. The Externals are also classified along with the Internals.

The **External Properties** (select the external item, right-click and select **Get Info**) has now the following content:

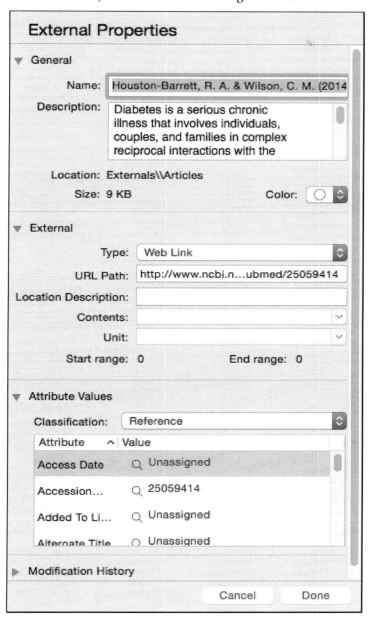

To reach the external file or the URL select the external item, right-click and select **Open External File** and you will normally be directed to the database and the current record, in our example PubMed health information database.

A New Source Classification

As mentioned above a source classification has been created when the EndNote import procedure took place. The name of the classification is *Reference* by default. The classification opens like any other classification by double-clicking on the item **Reference** located under **CLASSIFICATIONS** and the **Source Classifications** folder. Source items in **Internals//Articles** and **Externals//Articles** (both with and witout PDFs) have been classified.

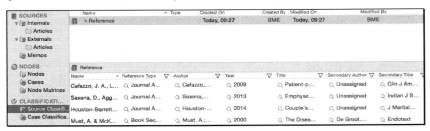

16. ABOUT QUESTIONNAIRES AND DATASETS

This section deals with data that originates from both multiple-choice questions and open-ended questions. In NVivo a Dataset is a Source Item in NVivo created when structured data is imported. Structured data is organized in records (rows) and fields (columns). The structured data formats that NVivo can import are Excel spreadsheets, tab-delimited text files and database-tables compatible with Microsoft's Access. A Dataset in NVivo is presented in a built-in reader that can display data in both a table format and in a form format. The reader makes it much easier to work on the computer and read and analyze data.

A Dataset has two types of fields (columns), namely Classifying and Codable.

Classifying is a field with demographic content of a quantitative nature, often the result of multiple choice questions. The data in these fields is expected to correspond to attributes and values.

Codable is a field with 'open ended content' like qualitative data. The data in these fields should typically be the subject of theme coding.

Datasets can only be created when data is imported. Data is arranged in the form of a matrix where rows are records and columns are fields. Typically, respondents are rows, columns are questions and cells are answers.

Importing Datasets

Structured data of any origin can be imported into NVivo so long as it meets the criteria described above:

1   Go to **Data | Import | Dataset**.
Default folder is **Internals**.
Go to 4.

alternatively

1   Under **SOURCES** open **Internals** or any of its subfolders.
2   Go to **Data | Import | Dataset**.
Go to 4.

alternatively

2   Click on any empty space in the List View.
3   Right-click and select **Import → Dataset...**

Tip: An easy way to convert an Excel worksheet to text is:
1. Select the whole worksheet
2. Copy
3. Open Notepad
4. Paste into Notepad
5. Save with a new name

With the filebrowser you will find the data file that you want to import. The file browser only allows Excel-files (.XLS and .XLSX) to be imported as Datasets. Click **[Open]**:

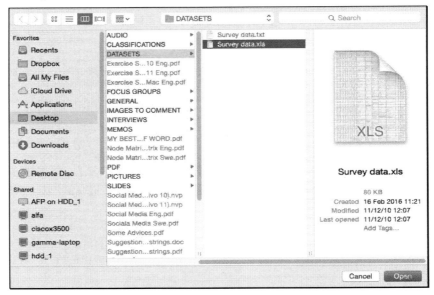

The **Import Dataset Assistant – Step 2** appears. The two buttons **[Survey data]** and **[variable explanations]** are the two sheets of the current workbook.

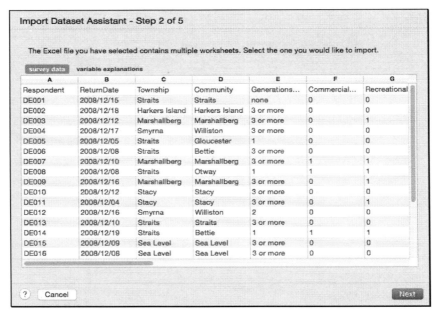

4 Select **[Survey data]** and then click **[Next]**.

158

The **Import Dataset Assistant – Step 3** appears:

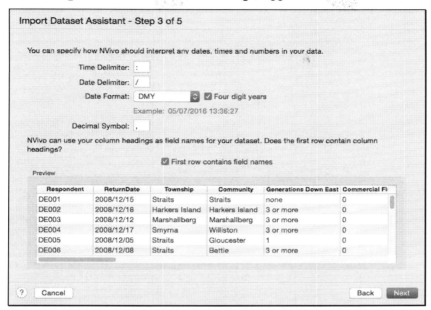

You can verify the Time and Date formats and the Decimal symbol against the information displayed in the **Preview** field.

It is important that the field names of imported data are only in the first row. Certain datasheets have field names in two rows and if so then the two rows must be merged. If you uncheck the option First row contains field names the row instead will contain column numbers.

5 Click [**Next**].

The **Import Dataset Assistant – Step 4** appears:

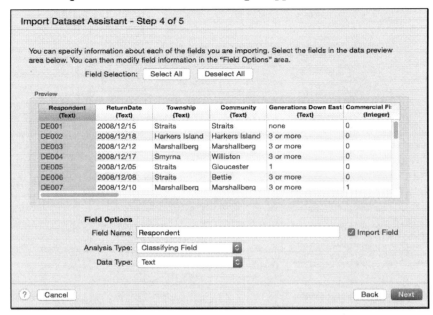

You must assign each column as either a *Codable Field* or as a *Classifying Field*. Select one column at a time by clicking the column head (or browse with [**Right**] or [**Left**] on the keyboard) in the Data Preview section. Use the options under Analysis Type. NVivo has suggested an analysis type for each column which you might modify. Unchecking the *Import Field* option for a certain column prevents its import.

5   Click [**Next**].

The **Import Dataset Assistant – Step 4** appears:

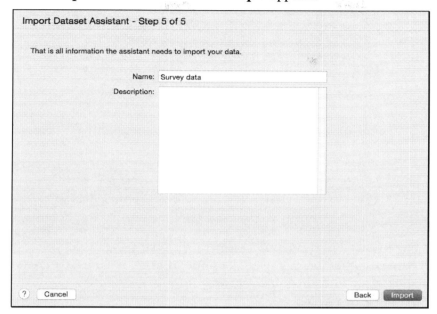

7   Type a name (compulsory) and a description (optional).
    Confirm with [**Import**].

A successful import creates a Dataset and when it opens it appears like this:

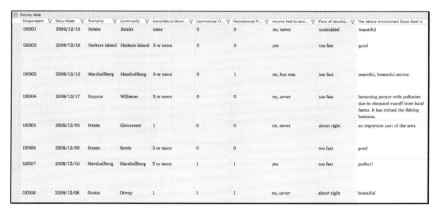

A Dataset cannot be edited nor can you create or delete rows or columns. The buttons down right are for browsing between pages of 100 records each. Columns with grey background are Classifying and columns with white background are Codable

Opening a Dataset

1. Under **SOURCES** open **Internals** or any of its subfolders.
2. Select the Dataset that you want to open.
3. Go to **Home | Item | Open**
   or right-click and select **Open**
   or double-click on the Dataset.

Exporting Datasets

Datasets cannot be exported like other Project Items.

Coding Datasets

Coding Datasets applies all the common rules: select text in codeable fields, right-click and select **Code Selection → At Existing Nodes or Cases...** or **At New Node.../Case...**

All coding in a Dataset can be explored like in other Project Items including quering, coding stripes and highlighting.

However, there is an imperfection for Datasets regarding Spread Coding as we have described on page 138. Not applicable.

Autocoding Datasets

Autocoding Datasets is the opportunity to use Nodes to provide a structure to your Dataset content when you import it into NVivo.

1. Select a Dataset in the List View.
2. Go to **Analyze | Coding | Auto Code**
   or right-click and select **Autocode...**

The **Auto Code Dataset Assistant – Step 1** appears:

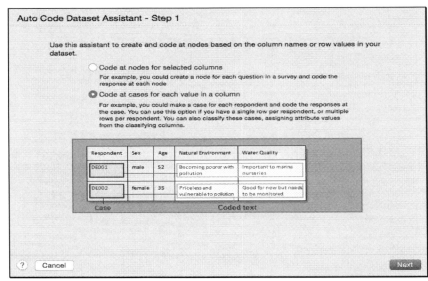

3. Select *Code at cases for each value in a column,* then click [**Next**].

The **Auto Code Dataset Assistant – Step 2** appears:

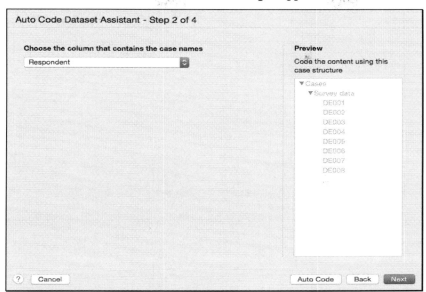

We select *Respondent* from the ***Choose the column that contains the case names*** drop-down list. The case hierarchy is shown in the preview box.

4   Click [**Next**].

The **Auto Code Dataset Assistant – Step 3** appears:

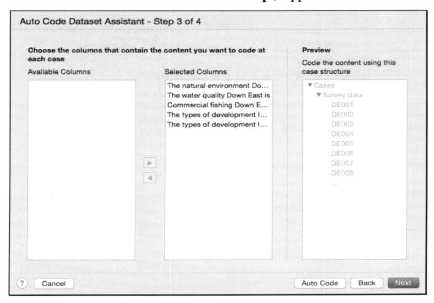

In this dialog box you can accept the selection of columns or deselect columns by bringing them to the Available Columns box.

6   Click [**Next**].

The **Auto Code Dataset Assistant** – **Step 4** appears:

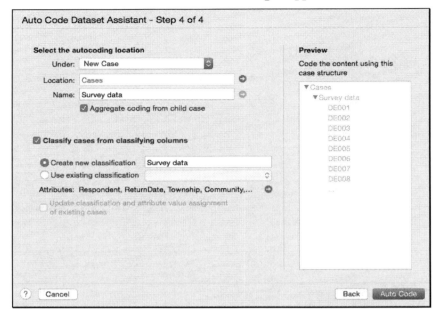

In this dialog box you can change the location of the cases to any existing case folder or parent case. Often it is adviseable to choose Aggregate here. You can also classify the cases already now by checking the option Classify cases from classifying columns.

7   Click **[Auto Code]**.

The cases created from this procedure look like this:

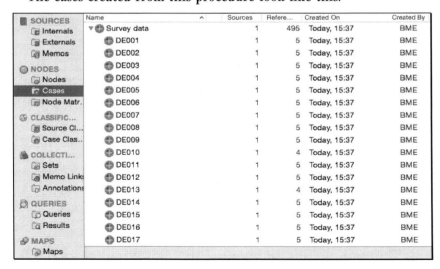

The case classification **Survey data** now looks like this::

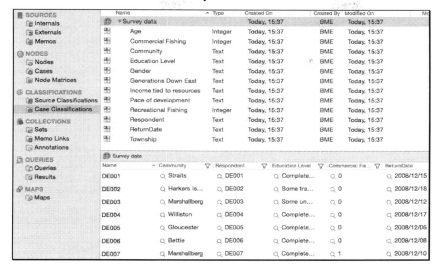

The next logical step would be to autocode our Dataset in relation to the columns we have classified as Codable. Each such column will constitute a theme node. We return once more to the Autocode command.

The **Auto Code Dataset Assistant – Step 1** appears:

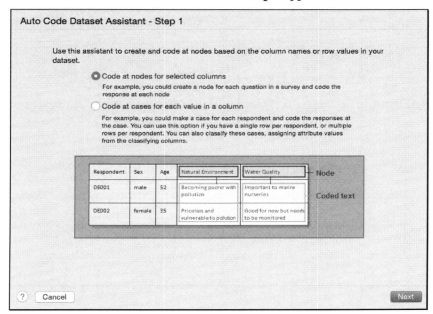

1. Select *Code at at nodes for selected columns,* then click [**Next**].

The **Auto Code Dataset Assistant – Step 2** appears:

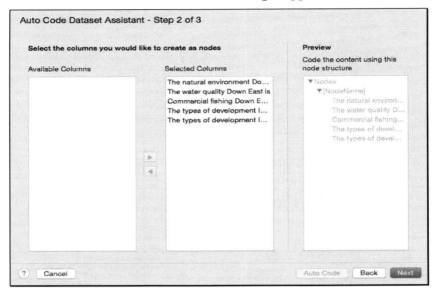

In this dialog box you can accept the selection of columns or deselect columns by bringing them to the Available Columns box.

2   Click [**Next**].

The **Auto Code Dataset Assistant – Step 3** appears:

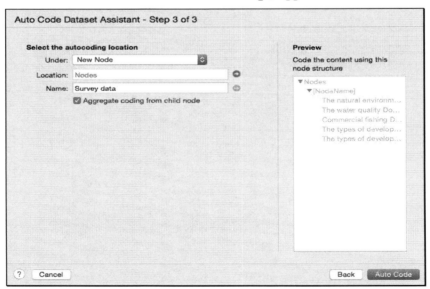

In this dialog box you can change the location of the nodes to any existing node folder or parent node. Often it is adviseable to choose Aggregate here.

3   Click [**Auto Code**].

The nodes created from this procedure look like this:

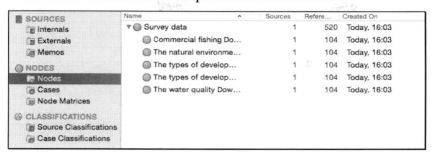

17. INTERNET AND SOCIAL MEDIA

Arguably the most significant upgrade for NVivo for Mac is the ability to import and handle data from internet such as web pages and social media sites like LinkedIn, Facebook, Twitter, and YouTube.

Introducing NCapture

NCapture is a browser plugin that is delivered and installed with NVivo. NCapture exports web content into files called *web data packages* (.NVCX file) that you will import into NVivo. NCapture allows you to export any website including the website's text, images and hyperlinks. Websites import into NVivo as PDF sources. NCapture also allows you to export data from LinkedIn, Facebook and Twitter. Social media data can also import into NVivo as a PDF source, but more importantly social media data can also be imported as an NVivo Dataset. Presently, NCapture is available as addins with Google Chrome, but other browsers may be available to work with NCapture as a part of future updates.

Exporting websites with NCapture

First open Chrome on a web-site you want to capture.
1. Select the **NCapture icon** on the right-hnd side of the toolbar of the web-browser:

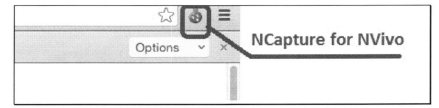

Importantly, you can export numerous web data packages during your online research. NVivo does not require you to import your web data until you're ready.

When you select to import a website to NVivo, the **Capture for NVivo** dialog box appears in the web-browser:

For websites, your Source Type will be Web Page as PDF by default as NVivo can currently only create website data packages that will be imported as PDF sources. But a variety of useful options are available for you to customize how your web data package can be imported into NVivo:

Source name will be the name of your new PDF source –the website's name will be the default here.

The *Description/Memo* tab allows you to type custom text that you want to add into *Description field* of the PDF Source Item or a newly created *linked Memo* with the same name as the Source Item. Which of these options works best for you will depend on your project – remember, linked memo content can be searched and coded; description field text cannot. Code at Nodes: You can type the names of any number of new or existing Nodes here. NCapture only has the ability to code web content at Nodes located in the Nodes folder. The imported PDF Source Item will be 100% coded at Nodes entered in the *Code at Nodes* field. When options have been completed, click **[Capture]**.

Importing Websites with NCapture

After NCapture exports your data, you will need to retrieve and import the newly created web data package (.nvcx) file(s). When you have returned to NVivo:
1. Go to **Data | Import | NCapture**
   Default folder is **Internals**.
   Go to 4.

alternatively
1. Under **SOURCES** open **Internals** or any of its subfolders.
2. Go to **Data | Import Ncapture**
   Go to 4.

alternatively
2. Click on any empty space the List View.
3. Right-click and select **Import → NCapture...**
   The **Import From:** dialog box appears:

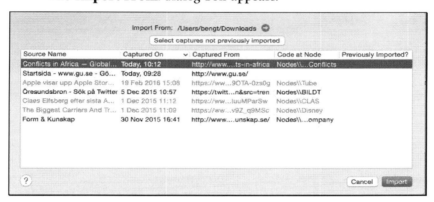

The recently captured item is on top of the list. Previously captured but not yet imported items are listed in bold. The default selection is All captures not previously imported. You can now select among the bold items which you want to import.
4. Click [**Import**].

First you will see the **PDF Properties** dialog box:

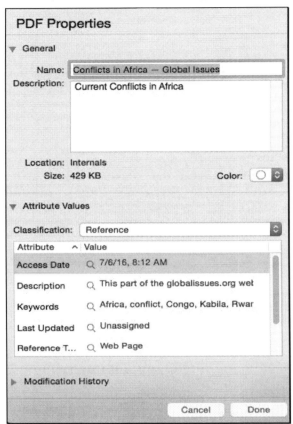

5   [**Cancel**] interrupts the import and [**Done**] completes the import.

The sample PDF Source item below is an export from the website 'Conflicts in Africa - Global Issues'. You'll notice that the webpage title is the same as the name of the PDF source file. Imported NCapture websites are classified with the Source Classification 'Reference'. Values are inserted by default for the following Attributes: Reference Type, Title, keywords, URL and Access Date. As you'll recall from our sample export image above, this entire PDF source will be coded at two Nodes, *Africa* and *Conflicts* and a linked memo will have been created sharing the PDF source's name, *Conflicts in Africa - Global Issues.*

Now you can open the source and hyperlinks are clickable like in any PDF item by using [⌘] + click.

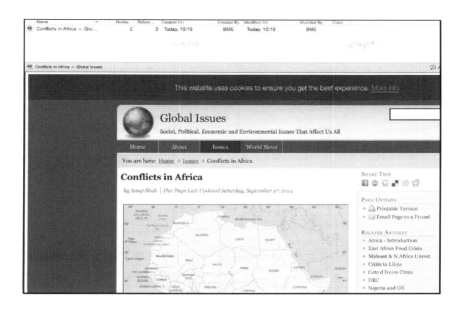

Social Media Data and NCapture

NCapture can also be used to capture a wealth of data from Facebook and Twitter. Social media web data packages can be created as PDF sources or Datasets, which will be the focus of our description below.

Due to each social media site's unique structure, NCapture captures different types of data from each site. While a summary of the complete functionality of Facebook, Twitter, and LinkedIn is beyond our purposes here, we will provide an explanation of the types of data you can capture from each site. Importantly, your ability to capture social media data is contingent on the privacy settings of the individual or group whose data you are interested in capturing (e.g., some Twitter users may require you to be their Follower before you can capture their Twitter data).

Importantly, you can use NCapture to gather social media data over a period of time and then easily update the data later. When you import web data packages containing social media data, by default, new data will be merged with old data so long as the original social media properties (e.g., hashtags, usernames, etc.) remains the same.

NCapture for Facebook Data

NCapture allows you to capture Facebook wall posts and data about their authors. Whether from an individual's Facebook wall (e.g., Allan McDougall), a Group wall (e.g., the Stockholm Sailing Club), or a Page wall (e.g., QSR International), NCapture can export wall posts, tags, photos, hyperlinks, link captions, link descriptions, number of 'likes', comments, comment 'likes', dates and times of posts and comments. Further, NCapture can capture authors' names, genders, birthdays, locations, relationship statuses, bios, religions, and hometowns.

NCapture for Twitter Data

NCapture allows you to capture Twitter tweets and data about their authors. Unlike Facebook, which is largely based on users being connected as 'friends' or as fans who 'like' a specific page, Twitter profiles and their attendant tweets are (typically) publically available. As a result, along with individual user streams, full Twitter searches can also be captured with NCapture. Whether for user streams or search results, NCapture can capture tweets along with their attendant usernames, mentions (usernames within tweets), hashtags (user-driven keywords), timestamps, locations, hyperlinks (if any), retweets (reposts by other users), and usernames of any 'retweeters'. Unlike NCapture's ability to capture demographic data from Facebook, NCapture for Twitter captures data associated with a user's influence level (or klout), such as number of tweets, number of followers, and the number of users they are following.

NCapture for LinkedIn Data

LinkedIn recently limited access to their web service (API), restricting the information available to apps like NCapture.

As a result, you can no longer capture a LinkedIn group discussion as a Dataset using NCapture.
This is out of QSR's control, but is something we will continue to monitor should LinkedIn change their policies in the future.

You can still capture a group discussion, and any other page in LinkedIn, as a PDF. Any LinkedIn group discussions captured previously can still be imported and analyzed in NVivo.

> **Tip:** Although you can't export LinkedIn users' profile data as a dataset with NCapture, you can still export user profiles as a PDF source. While unstructured, these PDF source can still be searched and coded after you import them into NVivo.

NCapture for YouTube

You can capture video clippings from YouTube as a Video item with or without comments or as a PDF.

Even though you can capture YouTube video items via NCapture, thiese items cannot be imported into NVivo for Mac as the functionality is not yet available:

Capturing Social Media Data with NCapture

Once you have found social media data that you need then activate NCapture from Google Chrome as described above. For social media web data packages, the default source type is a Dataset. You can choose between Dataset and PDF.

Like capturing websites with NCapture, when you capture social media data you can create an item description, linked memo, and Nodes. After completed the **NCapture** dialog box, click **[Capture]**.

Importing Social Media Data from NCapture

Now that you've captured your social media data to a web data package, it's time to import:
1. Go to **Data | Import | NCapture**.
   Default folder is **Internals**.
   Go to 4.

alternatively
1. Under **SOURCES** open **Internals** or any of its subfolders.
2. Go to **Data | Import | NCapture**.
   Go to 4.

alternatively
2. Click on any empty space in Area 3.
3. Right-click and select **Import → NCapture...**

First you will see the **Import From:** dialog box:

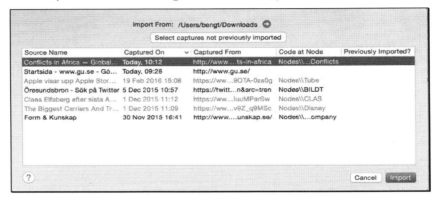

The recently captured item is on top of the list. Previously captured but not yet imported items are listed in bold. The default selection is All captures not previously imported. You can now select among the bold items which you want to import.
4. Click **[Import]**.

First you will see the **Dataset Properties** dialog box:

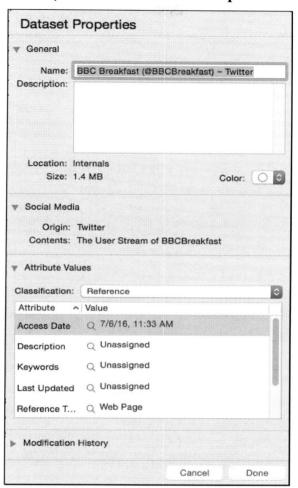

5   [**Cancel**] interrupts the import and [**Done**] completes the import.

The sample Dataset Source Item below is an export from Twitter. You'll notice the Dataset Source Item contains the LinkedIn group name. Imported NCapture social media data is classified with the Source Classification 'Reference'. Values are inserted by default for the following Attributes: Reference Type, Title, keywords, URL and Access Date.

Now you can open the Dataset:

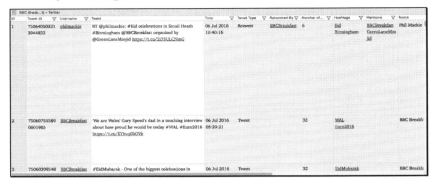

Analyzing Social Media Datasets

A number of exciting methods for analyzing social media Datasets exist in NVivo. Like any open Dataset source, you can search for patterns in your data by hiding, sorting, or filtering rows and columns. More advanced analysis functions such as Word Frequency Queries and Text Search Queries can offer insight into some themes in your data as well.

Autocoding a Dataset from Social Media

Autocoding a Dataset is described in detail in Chapter 16. The result of these autocoding procedures will be: Cases created from each TwitterID, a Classification for these cases with Attributes from each classifying column.

Nodes (Theme nodes) will be created from each codable column.

Installing NCapture

For Google Chrome:
1. Run Google Chrome.
2. Find the link with the installation guide on QSR's web page.
3. Follow the prompts to complete the installation.

Check your Version of NCapture

For Google Chrome:
Go to **Window → Extensions**
View the version number for **NCapture for NVivo** in the list.

18. USING ONENOTE WITH NVIVO

Using OneNote with NVivo is a significant update that we are very happy about! OneNote is popular, cloud-based, notetaking utility developed by Microsoft. It allows you to synchronize text-based, hand-written, or multimedia notes across all of your mobile devices. In February, 2015, Microsoft made the full version of OneNote completely free to all users.

OneNote turns your smartphone or tablet into an instant, cloud-based data collection device. You can use OneNote to write and organize notes on your work PC or record audio/video clips on their mobile devices. As soon as you make a change to your OneNote file, those changes will be reflected across all of your connected devices. Create a fieldnote, audio interview, or photograph and it will be waiting for you on your PC when you return to your office.

NVivo for Mac now allows users to import their OneNote content by selecting which pages they want to import. Pages are imported as document or PDF sources, however if the OneNote contains attachments NVivo will create new project items for each one—such as text, photo or video items. NVivo will also create a folder hierarchy that reflects the organizational structure of your OneNote notes, and notebooks.

Describing the functionality of OneNote is beyond our purposes here, we will provide an instruction how to capture data that is already stored on your OneNote account.

1. Go to **Data | Import | OneNote Data**
   Default folder is **Internals**.
   Go to 4.

alternatively

1. Under **SOURCES** open **Internals** or any of its subfolders.
2. Go to **Data | Import | OneNote Data.**
   Go to 4.

alternatively

2. Click on any empty space in the List View.
3. Right-click and select **Import → OneNote...**

In each case the following dialog box appears:

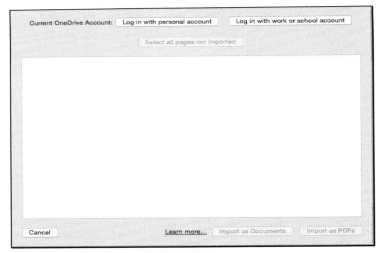

After logging in with your personal account it may look like this:

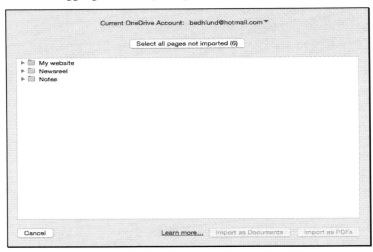

First you will see the various Notebooks that you have created in OneNote.

When clicking on [**Select all pages not imported**] you will see all your subfolders and pages like this:

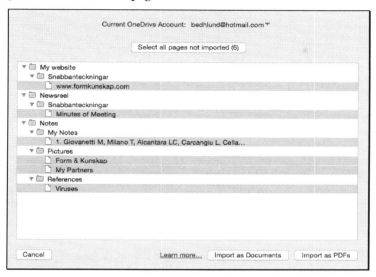

4   Now you may select or deselect any pages for you import. You may also choose between [**Import as Documents**] or [**Import as PDFs**].

Importing as Documents offers an option to edit the documents once imported to NVivo.

The import creates subfolders mirroring the various notebooks and the pages are source items. Now you may proceed with you coding and linking procedures and prepare for your analysis.

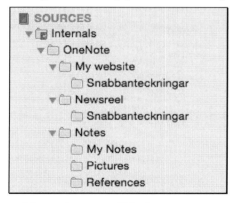

If you have modified your notes in OneNote and want to import an updated note, you need to manually select that page in the import dialog and import again. In NVivo you will have an updated item with same name and a suffix like (2) after the name.

In order to import material from OneNote, you must have a Microsoft OneDrive account—this is Microsoft's free, online, cloud-based file storage service. You and your team can create as many OneDrive accounts as you need. OneNote allows you and your team to share notes as needed. In some cases, NVivo for Mac may be unable to find notes and notebooks that were shared with you.

If you have more than one account that you use to access different OneNote notebooks, you can log into a different account. For example, if you are currently logged in with your personal account, then in the dialog, next to *Current OneDrive Account*, select **Log in with different personal account...** or **Log in with work or school account**.

19. COLLABORATING WITH NVIVO

As technology and interdisciplinary facilitate more and more complex qualitative studies, teamwork structures and procedures become increasingly important. NVivo allows several users to use the same project file provided that the file is opened by one user at a time. Alternatively, each member can work with his/her own project file that can be merged into a master file at a certain predefined occasion. The focus of this chapter is on how a team can operate using a single project file. The first half of this chapter explains some collaboration tools features in NVivo. The second half explains some general insights on collaborating with NVivo.

Collaborating on the same NVivo project can be arranged in a number of ways:
- Team members can use the same data but each individual creates his/her Nodes and codes accordingly – perhaps importing to a master project later.
- Team members use different data but use a common Node structure.
- Team members use both the same data and a common Node structure.

In cases where individual team members plan to merge their analytic progress into a master project file, merging projects is described on page 43. Review the options of the **Import Project** dialog box to find out how it can suite your needs. If Nodes with same names need to merge you can select Merge into existing item. Remember that Nodes and other items must have the same name and must be located on the same level of the folder structure before they can be merged successfully. Further, the contents of the Source Items must be identical.

The most important feature in NVivo for Mac for collaborative data analysis is:
- Coding Comparison Queries for comparing two coders working with the same sources and Nodes. This is an important option that improves a project's validity and quantifies inter-rate reliability.

Current User

An important concept for teamwork in NVivo is the **Current User**. In **NVivo → Preferences** or [⌘] + [,] and the **Application Preferences** dialog box, the **General** section identifies the current user. When a project is open you can change the current user. However, it is not possible to leave the Name and Initial boxes empty.

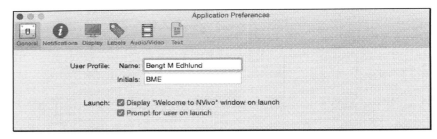

If you select the option Prompt for user on launch then the dialog box is prompted each time NVivo is started:

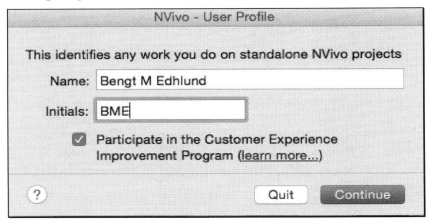

All users who have worked on the project are listed in **File → Project Properties** or **[Shift] + [⌘] + [,]** and in the **Users** section:

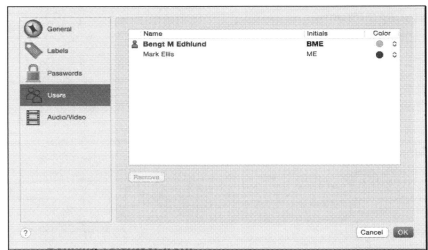

The current user is written in bold. The small triangle in the left column indicates the user who created the current project.

Initials are used to identify all Project Items created or modified by a certain user.

Coding Comparison Query

For projects interested in studying inter-rater reliability it is possible to compare how two people or two groups of people have coded the same material. This is possible provided that the same source material and the same Node structure have been used:

- Go to **Query | Create | Coding Comparison**.
  Default folder is **Queries**.
  Go to 4.

alternatively

1. Under **QUERIES** open **Queries** or any of its subfolders.
2. Go to **Query | Create | Coding Comparison**.
   Go to 4.

alternatively

2. Click on any empty space in the List View.
3. Right-click and select **New Query → Coding Comparison**

The **Unsaved Query** dialog box appears:

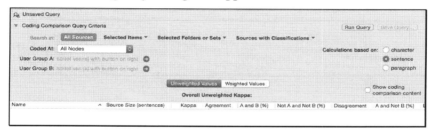

4. Define User group A and B with the [⊙]-buttons which give access to all users that have been working in the project.
5. The **Search in:** drop-down list determines the source items that will be compared.
6. The **Coded At:** drop-down list determines the Nodes or Cases that will be compared.
7. Select one of the options *Unweighted Values* or *Weighted Values.*

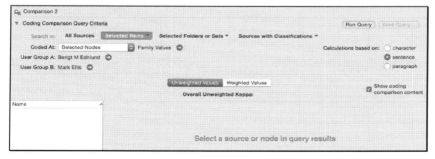

8. Save the query with [**Save Query...**].

9   Run the query with [**Run Query**].

The result (preview, which cannot be saved) is for the combination of selected sources items and selected nodes:

Provided that you have checked the option *Show coding comparison content* the result can look like this:

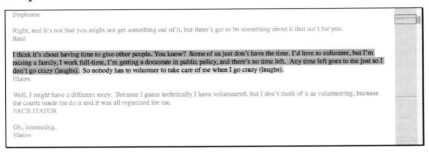

The percentage agreement columns indicate the following values:
- **Agreement** = sum of columns **A and B** and **Not A and Not B**.
- **A and B** = the percentage of data item content coded to the selected Node by both Project User Group A and Project User Group B.
- **Not A and Not B** = the percentage of data item content coded by neither Project User Group A and Project User Group B.
- Disagreement Column = sums of columns A and Not B and B and Not A.
- **A and Not B** = the percentage of data item content coded by Project User Group A and not coded by Project User Group B.
- **B and Not A** = the percentage of data item content coded by Project User Group B and not coded by Project User Group A.

Tips for Teamwork

Based on our years of experience working with hundreds of qualitative researchers using NVivo, we offer our colleagues the following tips for collaborating with NVivo:

- Appoint **an NVivo coordinator** for the research project.
- Set up **file name protocols**, read-only, storage locations, backup locations, file distribution and archiving.
- Set up **rules for audio and video files** like file formats and file distribution. For example, should you use embedded items or external files?
- Set up a **Node strategy**. Such a strategy can be communicated in a number of ways. It is easy to make a Node template in the form of a project without Source Items. Each Node should have 'instructions' written in the Node's Description field (max 512 characters) or in the form of a linked Memo, which is easier to write, read, print and code. The Node template can be distributed to team-members, saved with a new name and developed into a project in its own right. Importantly, the Node template's structure must not be modified by users. When new ideas are evolved, users should instead create new Nodes in addition to the Node template and create Memo Links.
- Determine how **Case Classifications** and **Source Classifications** will be applied. Such Nodes can be interviewees or other research items like places, professions, products, organizations, phenomena. In some situations it is useful to work with different classifications.
- Set up **rules for the master project** including protocols for merging and updating. Define a new project with a new name that clearly indicates that it is a merged project. Possibly a new set of user names will be defined for this purpose. Import one partial project at a time with **Import Project** and the option 'Merge into existing item'. Items with same name and same location will be merged.
- Hold periodic **team meetings** for the project. Such meetings should compare and analyze data (as described in this chapter), summarize discussions, and make decisions. Distribute minutes from each meeting.
- Assuming that the work has come to a stage where different members have submitted contributions to the project, make sure that the team has the standardized **usernames** when they work with their respective parts.

Continuing to Work on a Merged Project

After exploring a merged project you have two options to proceed:
- Each user continues with the original individual projects and at a certain point of time you make a complete new merger – perhaps archiving the original merger.
- Each user continues to work on the merged project and archives the original individual portions.

We recommend continuing with the first option up to a certain point and then, if the team agrees, deciding to focus on the merged project later.

A Note on Cloud-computing

Some researchers we have worked with use cloud-based file sharing services like Dropbox, SkyDrive and Google Drive as a working solution for collaborating on an NVivo Project. These services allow changes to the NVivo project file to be made across several computers using the 'cloud'. We recommend you turn off the live syncing features of these programs while you are running NVivo. We have been contacted by a number of colleagues and clients who have lost data while simultaneously using NVivo and syncing its attendant (.nvp) file. Again, cloud-based utilities can be useful for team collaboration, but taking the proper precautions can avoid costly loss of analysis time due to software crashes.

When you need to access a project file stored on any cloud service either copy the file to your local drive or create a new project and import the project file. Never open a project file from a USB memory or any cloud service.

A Note on NVivo Server

NVivo manufacturer QSR International has developed a collaborative software solution called NVivo Server. Presently the NVivo Server allows only Nvivo for Windows to be connected. Projects that are stored in NVivo Server can be considerably larger, up to 100 GB or more provided storage space is available. NVivo Server allows multiple users to work on the same project from different computers simultaneously. While useful, in our experience the logistical challenges associated with working on a server have kept our colleagues and clients from using this tool. While we support NVivo server, it is beyond the purposes of this book to describe it. Feel free to follow contact us directly if you and your team have any interest in NVivo Server.

20. VISUALIZATIONS

Maps, charts and diagrams are useful tools when a project is developing or when a project is ready to begin reporting findings. Such visualizatosn present ideas and theories visually. In a research team, those are also useful for team meetings. NVivo for Mac offers four types of visualizations: Mind Maps, Hierarchy Charts, Explore Diagrams, and Comparison Diagrams.

Mind Maps

Creating a Mind Map

A Mind Map reflects what you think about a single topic and is usually created quickly or spontaneously.

At the beginning of your project you might use a Mind Map to explore your expectations or initial theories. Later on, Mind Maps can help to confirm the structure of your nodes.

    1   Go to **Explore | Visualizatons | Mind Map**.
         Default folder is **Maps**.
         Go to 4.

alternatively

    1   Under **MAPS** open **Maps** or any of its Subfolders.
    2   Go to **Explore | Visualizations | Mind Map**.
         Go to 4.

alternatively

    2   Click on an empty space in the List View.
    3   Right-click and select **New Mind Map**

The **Mind Map Properties** dialog box appears:

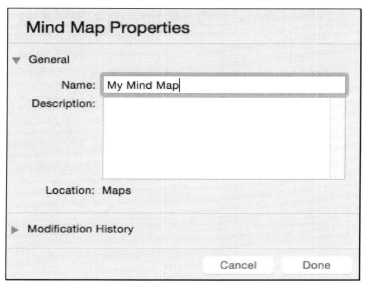

4   Type a name (compulsory) and a description (optional), then [**Done**].

A new window appears in the Detail View:

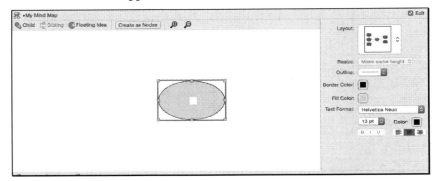

5   Select the main idea, right-click and select **Insert Child Idea**.

This image shows two added Child Ideas:

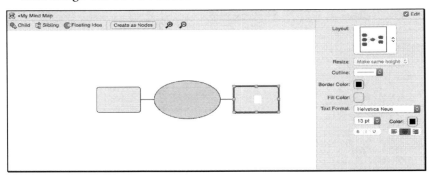

6   Select a child idea, right-click and select **Insert Sibling Idea**.

This image shows an added sibling idea.

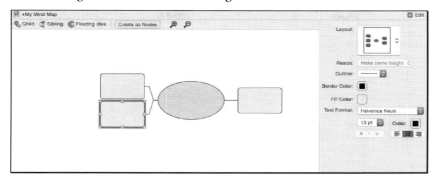

You can insert text in the symbols by selecting, right-click and select **Edit Label**. Changing fonts, font attribute, color and size you need to select text and use the right layout panel:

A Floating Idea is inserted by going by right-clicking in the Detail View and select **Insert Floating Idea**.

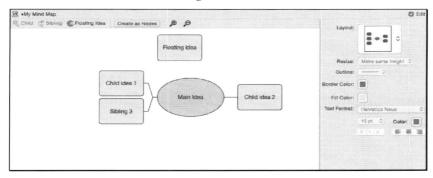

Ideas can also be moved around in a map by using normal **Cut** (or **Copy**) and **Paste** commands. When you paste on any idea the item (copied or cut) will become a new child idea.

If you want to create nodes based on your Mind Map you need to right-click on your mind map and select **Create As Nodes**. First you select the folder or the parent node which will be the location for the new nodes based on your current Mind Map:

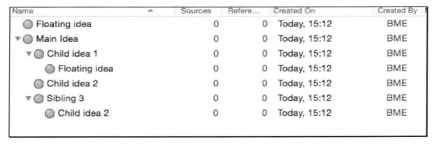

Layout

You can modify the layout of a map manually by moving any item with the mouse or drag in a corner of a selection to change the size or the proportions between height and width. The connectors between items will adopt as were they elastic.

There are a few layout templates available in NVivo. They can be applied by going to the right layout panel and select one of the templates:

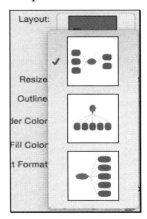

You can also make any selected items equal in size according to alternatives from the **Resize** dropdown list in the right layout panel:

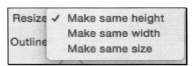

The first selected item becomes the model for the then selected items.

Deleting Graphical Items
1   Select one or more graphical items.
2   Go to **Home | Editing | Delete**
    or right-click and select **Delete**
    or the [←] key.

Exporting Maps
1   Open a Mind Map
2   Go to **Data | Export | Items**
    or right-click and select **Export Map.**
3   Decide file name and location. The possible file formats are: .PDF, .PNG, .JPG, .BMP, .GIF or .TIFF.

You can also copy the whole map or selected items and then go to **Home | Clipboard | Copy** or right-click the map and select **Copy**.

Hierarchy Charts

Hierarchy Charts makes it possible to visualize how source items and nodes are coded and classified and hierarchically organized with qualitative comparisons.

1 Go to **Explore | Visualizations | Hierarchy Chart**.
Any default Hierarchy Chart will appear.

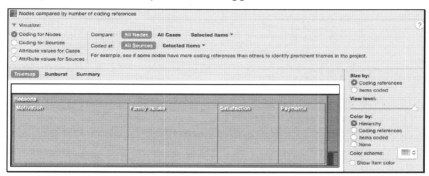

Here you can first decide if you want to study *Coding for Nodes* or *Coding for Sources* or *Attribute values for Cases* or *Attribute values Sources*. We accept to analyze nodes. Click [**Next...**].

Coding for Nodes

When we select Coding for Nodes and with the button [**Selected Items**] we select a node called Reasons for Volunteering the Hierarchy Chart in *Treemap* mode will look like this:

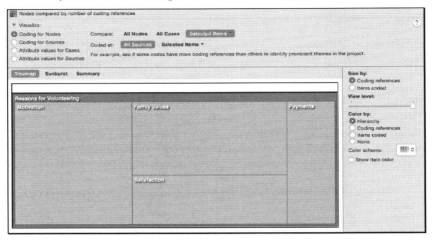

In this example the size of each region reflects the number of coding references.

As an alternative to the Treemap view you can also select view mode Sunburst:

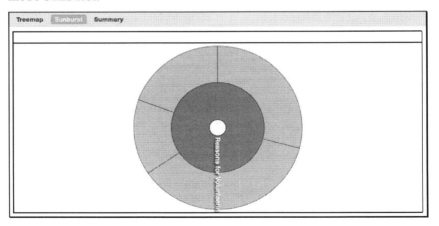

You can also start by selecting one or more nodes or cases, right-click and select **Visualize → Hierarchy Chart Of Nodes** or go to **Explore | Visualizations | Hierarchy Chart**.

Coding for Sources

When you want to study Sources and their coding, then you select *Coding for Sources* from the default Hierarchy Chart and then all sources will be shown. Using the **[Selected Items]** in the alternative *Coding for Nodes* you select the Sources you want to study.

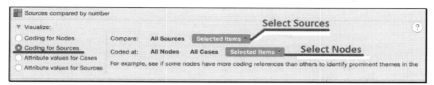

When you have selected the sources you want to study the result may look like this:

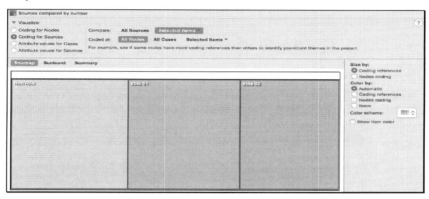

Then you can go further and specify the node or nodes that you want to analyse. By pointing at a region a text bubble will shoew the numer of nodes and the nunber of coding references.

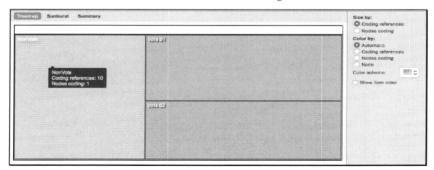

The size of the regions reflects either the number of coding references or the number of nodes coding depending on your setting in the rightmost panel. Here you can also decide upon the color scheme.

An alternative when analysing sources is starting by selecting two or more sources, right-click and select **Visualize → Hierarchy Chart Of Sources** or go to **Explore | Visualizations | Hierarchy Chart**.

Attribute values for Cases

Another setting is when you want to study a specific Attribute value for selected Cases classified by a Case Classification. Then you select the option *Attribute values for Cases* and in this example we select the Attribute *Age Group*.

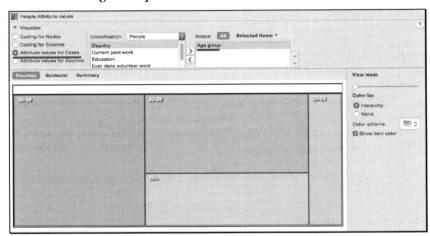

The *Sunburst* view looks like this:

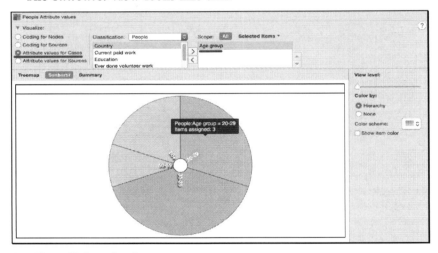

Attribute Values for Sources

This setting is used when you want to study a specific Attribute value for selected Sources classified by a Source Classification. Then you select the option *Attribute values for Sources* and you follow the corresponding procedure as for Cases above.

Exporting Charts

Charts are not permantent project items that are stored in NVivo. Such items need to be exported and saved outside NVivo.

1. Display an Hierachy Chart.
2. Go to **Data | Export | Items**
   or right-click and select **Export Hierarchy Chart...**
3. Decide name and location. The file formats are .PDF, .JPG, .BMP, or .TIFF.

You can also copy the whole chart and then go to **Home | Clipboard | Copy** or right-click the chart and select **Copy**.

Explore Diagrams

This type of diagram is a dynamic preview offering a visual analysis of a selected project item and its connections to all other items. Dynamic means that the diagram is updated as soon as any item is modified and preview means that such diagram is created and not saved unless it is exported and saved in any external format.

1. Select *one* item (Source, Node or Case) in the List View that you want to analyze.
2. Go to **Explore | Visualizations | Explore Diagram**
   or right-click and select **Visualize → Explore Diagram**.

The following diagram appears:

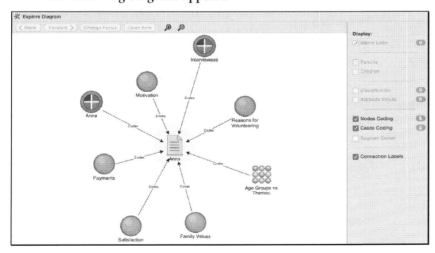

In the right-most panel you can select or de-select Nodes Coding, Cases Coding or Connection Labels. The modification takes effect promptly.

Depending on the choice of item to study you will also have the options to show Memo Links, Parents, Children, Classification and Attribute Values.

You can select which type of connected items you want to study furher, right-click and select **Change Focus**. Then a new diagram is shown with the newly selected item in focus:

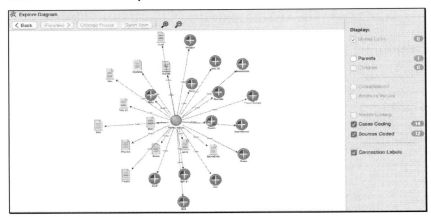

Now you can alternate between these two diagrams using the [**Back**] and {**Forward**] buttons on left side of the top bar. You can also right-click and alternatively select **Back** or **Forward**.

From these diagrams you can open any item by going to **Home | Item | Open** or right-click and select **Open Item...**

You can also go on in your analysis and select again a new item and **Change Focus**. With this option you can go backwards or forwards in many steps.

Exporting Explore Diagrams
Explore Diagrams are not permanent project items that are stored in NVivo. Such items need therefore to be exported and saved outside NVivo.
1. Go to **Data | Export | Items**
   or right-click and select **Export Diagram...**
2. Decide name and location. The file formats are .PDF, .JPG, .BMP, or .TIFF.

You can also copy the whole chart or seleted items and then go to **Home | Clipboard | Copy** or right-click the chart and select **Copy**.

Comparison Diagrams

To create a Comparison Diagram, use the Ribbon menu and select
Explore | Visualizations | Compare Diagram → <select>

The <select> options are: Compare Sources..., Compare Nodes..., Compare Cases... or Compare Selected Items.

Whichever option you would like to visualize, Comparison Diagrams must be *two items of same type*.

In this example, we compare the two case nodes that represent research participants, Anna and Ken. First we navigate to **Compare Nodes** and select the case nodes for *Anna* and *Ken*. The resulting Comparison Diagram looks like this:

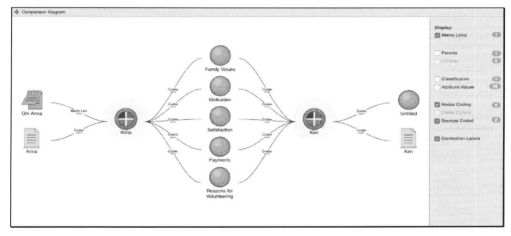

In the Comparison Diagram's right-side control panel, you can select or deselect diagram features.

When you want to explore an item from the diagram in more detail, right-click any item and select one of the following options: **Open Item...**, **Get Info**, **Select All**, **Copy**, and **Export Diagram...**

NVivo for Mac also allows you to visually modify a diagram's layout by simply dragging items with the mouse. Item connectors behave like they are elastically glued to diagram items—we love this feature and encourage you to try it out for yourself!

Importantly, the diagram is a preview and cannot be stored as a project item. However, using the Export option you can choose among the following file formats: .PDF, .PNG, .JPG, .BMP, .GIF, or TIFF.

As with other NVivo diagrams, you can select items or all items with right-click and **Select All** or [⌘] + [A], copy with right-click and **Copy** or [⌘] +[C] and then paste into any third party application, such as Keynote, Word or PowerPoint.

21. HELP FUNCTIONS IN NVIVO

An integral part of NVivo is the variety of help and support functionality for users.

Help Documents Online

1 Go to the **Help** menu and you will find the following options or use the [?] symbol in the upper right corner of the various dialog boxes:

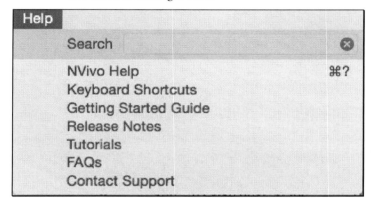

Search

In the **Search** textbox you can type any subject term and a meny will show like this and the each alternative will directly point at a ribbon menu alternative.

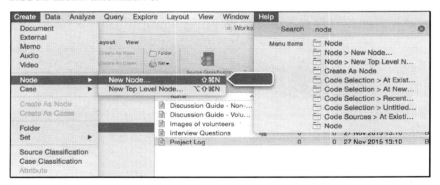

NVivo Help

The initial view for Online **NVivo Help** which you also reach directly with [⌘] + [?] is:

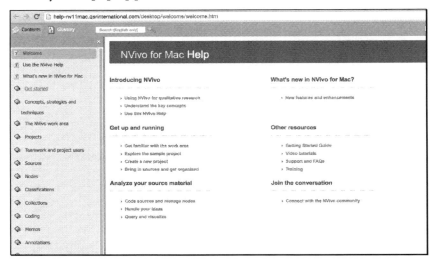

Keyboard Shortcuts

A complete list of shortcuts will be displayed.

Getting Started Guide

This is a PDF document with tips and suggestions how to start up and organize a project.

Release Notes

A list of update releases and information and comments on news and technical issues.

Tutorials

NVivo has some tutorials in the form of video clips.

FAQs

This option leads to QSRs website and as for local support you are also welcome to contact Bengt Edhlund, one of the autors of this book. See below.

Support and Technical Issues

As a holder of this book you are welcome to contact **support@formkunskap.com** or Skype **bengt.edhlund** in any matter that has to do with installation problems or user procedures as described in this book.

In case of performance disturbances like NVivo unintentionally stops, an error log is created automatically. The log files are by default stored in the Library folder under Logs\\NVivo.
1. Open **Finder**
2. Click **Go** in the Mac menu
3. Press the option key, [**alt**]
4. Go to the folder **Library\\Logs\\NVivo**
5. The log file is named **log-xxxxxx.txt** with its creation date

It is a text file and in case you need technical assistance you may be asked to forward such error log file to QSR Support or to the local representative for analysis.

Screen Shots

In certain support matters it is very helpful for an effective feedback when you send a screen shot to the support management. In the below described methods the result is a PNG-file located on the desktop which can be pasted into other applications like Word. You can interrupt any time with the [**esc**]-key. The options are:

Screen Shot of the whole Screen
[⌘] + [**Shift**] + [3]

Screen Shot of a region of the Screen
[⌘] + [**Shift**] + [4]

The cursor becomes a cross and you hold down the mouse key and mark a region.

Screen Shot of a Window
[⌘] + [**Shift**] + [4]

The cursor becomes a cross and then you press [**Space**]. The cursor now becomes a camera that you can place in the window in question and you click the mouse or corresponding action.

Software Versions and Service Packs

You should always be aware of the software version and Service Pack that you use. A Service Pack is an additional software patch that could carry bug fixes, improvements and new features. Service Packs are free for licensees of a certain software version.

1   Go to **NVivo → About NVivo**.

The image shows the software version and installed Service Pack:

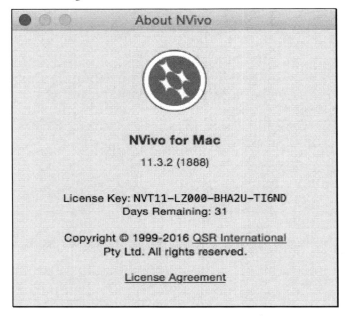

It is a good idea to check for updates frequently.

1   Go to **NVivo → Check for Updates...**.

This messaage confirms that your NVivo for Mac is up-to-date.

22. GLOSSARY

This is a list of the most common words, terms, and descriptions that are used in this book or during our lectures and workshops. Topics included in this Glossary does not necessarily mean that they are supported by the present version of NVivo for Mac.

Advanced Find	Search names of Project items like Source items, Memos or Nodes. Use **Find Bar - Advanced Find.**
Aggregate	Aggregate means that a certain Node in any hierarchical level accumulates the logical sum of all its nearest Child Nodes.
Annotation	A note linked to an element of a Source item. Similar to a conventional footnote.
Attribute	A variable that is used to describe individual Source items and Nodes. Example: age group, gender, education.
Autocoding	An automatic method to code documents using names of the paragraph styles.
Boolean Operator	The conventional operators AND, OR or NOT used to create logical search expressions applying Boolean algebra.
Case Node	A Case Node is a member of a group of Nodes which are classified with Attributes and Values reflecting demographic or descriptive data. Case Nodes can be people (Interviewees), places or any group of items with similar properties.
Casebook	Definition used in NVivo 8 corresponding to Classification Sheet in later versions of NVivo.
Classification	A collection of Attributes for Source items or Nodes.
Classification Sheet	A matrix overview of the attributes and values of Source items or Nodes.
Cluster Analysis	Cluster analysis or clustering is the assignment of a set of observations into subsets (called *clusters*) so that observations in the same cluster are similar in some sense. Clustering is a method of unsupervised learning, and a common technique for statistical data analysis used in many fields, including machine learning, data mining, pattern recognition, image analysis, information retrieval, and bioinformatics.

Coding	The work that associates a certain element of a Source item at a certain Node.
Coding Stripe	Graphical representation of coding in a Source item.
Coding Queries	A method to construct a query by using combinations of Nodes or Attribute values.
Compound Queries	A method to construct a query by using combinations of various query types.
Concept Map	A Concept Map is a free-form visualization made up of different shapes and connectors. Shapes represent concepts (ideas, people, or data). The connectors between the shapes articulate links such as *this causes...*, *this requires...* or *this contributes to...*
Coverage	The fraction of a Source item that has been coded at a certain Node.
Dataset	A structured matrix of data arranged in rows and columns. Datasets can be created from imported Excel spreadsheets or captures social media data.
Dendrogram	A tree-like plot where each step of hierarchical clustering is represented as a fusion of two branches of the tree into a single one. The branches represent clusters obtained at each step of hierarchical clustering.
Discourse Analysis	In semantics, discourses are linguistic units composed of several sentences — in other words, conversations, arguments or speeches. Discourse Analysis studies how texts can be structured and how its elements are interrelated.
Document	An item in NVivo that is usually imported from a Source document.
Dropbox	A cloud-based software solution that allows file syncing across several computers.
EndNote	A powerful and convenient reference handling software tool.
Ethnography	The science that examines characteristics of different cultural groups.
Evernote	A popular cloud-based notetaking platform that creates text and voice memos.

Facebook	A social networking platform where users can become 'friends' and post content on one another's personal page ('walls'). Social groups are also available in Facebook (pages).
Filter	A function that limits a selection of values or items in order to facilitate the analysis of large amounts of data.
Find Bar	A toolbar immediately above the List View.
Focus Group	A selected, limited group of people that represents a larger population.
Folder	A folder that is created by NVivo is a virtual folder but has properties and functions largely like a normal Windows folder.
Framework	A data matrix that allows you to easily view and summarize areas of your data you wish to more closely explore.
Grounded Theory	Widely recognized method for qualitative studies where theories emerge from data rather than a pre-determined hypothesis.
Grouped Find	A function for finding items that have certain relations to each other.
Hushtag	A 'keywording' convention that places a number sign (#) before a term in order to allow text-based searches to distinguish searchable keywords from standard discourse (see also, Twitter).
Hyperlink	A link to an item outside the NVivo-project. The linked item can be a file or a web site.
In Vivo Coding	In Vivo coding is creating a new Node when selecting text and then using the *In Vivo* command. The Node name will become the selected text (max 256 characters) but the name (and location) can be changed later.
Items	All items that constitutes a project. Items are Sources, Nodes, Classifications, Queries, Results, and Maps.
Jaccard's Coefficient	The **Jaccard index**, also known as the **Jaccard similarity coefficient** (originally coined *coefficient de communauté* by Paul Jaccard), is a statistic used for comparing the similarity and diversity of sample sets

Kappa Coefficient	**Cohen's kappa coefficient, (K),** is a statistical measure of inter-rater agreement. It is generally thought to be a more robust measure than simple percent agreement calculation since **K** takes into account the agreement occurring by chance. Cohen's kappa coefficient measures the agreement between two raters who each classify N items into C mutually exclusive categories. If the raters are in complete agreement then **K** = 1. If there is no agreement among the raters (other than what would be expected by chance) then **K** ≤ 0.
LinkedIn	A professional social networking site where users become 'connections' and participate in group discussions in 'groups'.
Matrix Coding Query	The method to construct queries in a matrix form where contents in each cell are the result of a row and a column combined with a certain operator.
Medline	The world's most popular health research database.
Memo Link	Only *one* Memo Link can exist from an item to a memo.
Memo	A text document that could be linked from *one* Source item or from *one* Node.
MeSH	MeSH (Medical Subject Headings), the terminology or controlled vocabulary used in PubMed and associated information sources.
Mind Map	A Mind Map reflects what you think about a single topic and is usually created quickly or spontaneously. At the beginning of your project you might use a mind map to explore your expectations or initial theories.

Mixed Methods	My thoughts on mixed methods include two aspects. First is the integration of survey, test, rating, demographic data with qualitative media (and all interaction with those media in terms of excerpting and tagging). When done well, database queries can draw upon all data points in filtering, creating data visualizations to explore pattern, and basic retrieval. The second is the various ways of quantifying qualitative data in terms of creating new descriptor variables and the scaling or indexing of coded content across meaningful dimensions.
NFS	**Network File System (NFS)** is a distributed file system protocol originally developed by Sun Microsystems in 1984, allowing a user on a client computer to access files over a computer network much like local storage is accessed.
Node	Often used in the context of a 'container' of selected topics or themes. A Node contains pointers to whole documents or selected elements of documents relevant to the specific Node. Nodes can be organized hierarchically.
OCR	Optical Character Recognition, a method together with scanning making it possible to identify characters not only as an image.
OneNote	Microsoft's cloud-based notetaking platform that creates text and voice memos.
Pearson Correlation Coefficient	A type of correlation coefficient that represents the relationship between two variables that are measured on the same interval or ratio scale.
Phenomenology	A method which is descriptive, thoughtful, and innovative and from which you might verify your hypothesis.
Project	The collective denomination of all data and related work.
Project Map	Graphical representation of Project items and their relations.
PubMed	A popular health research database (cf. Medline).

Qualitative Research	Research with data originating from observations, interviews, and dialogs that focuses on the views, experiences, values, and interpretations of participants.
Quantitative Research	Research that collects data through measurements and conclusions through calculations and statistics.
Ranking	The organization of results according to ascending or descending relevance.
RefWorks	A popular reference handling software tool.
Relationship	A Node that defines a relation between two Project items. A relationship is always characterized by a certain relationship type.
Relationship Type	A concept (often a descriptive verb) that defines a relationship or dependence between two Project items.
Relevance	Relevance in a result of a query is a measure of success or grade of matching. Relevance may be calculated as the number of hits in selected sections of the searched item.
Research Design	A plan for the collection and study of data so that the desired information is reached with sufficient reliability and a given theory can be verified or rejected in a recognized manner.
Result	A result is the answer to a query. A result may be shown as *Preview* or saved as a *Node*.
Saving Queries	The possibility to save queries in order to re-run or to modify them.
See Also Link	A link established between two items. A See Also Link is created from a certain area or text element of an item to a selected area or the whole of another item.
Service Pack	Software updates that normally carry bug fixes, performance enhancements, and new features.
Set	A subset or 'collection' of selected Project Items. A saved set can be displayed as a list of shortcuts to these Project Items.

Sociogram	A **sociogram** is a graphic representation of social links that a person has. It is a graph drawing that plots the structure of interpersonal relations in a group situation. Sociograms were developed by Jacob L. Moreno to analyze choices or preferences within a group. They can diagram the structure and patterns of group interactions. A sociogram can be drawn on the basis of many different criteria: Social relations, channels of influence, lines of communication etc.
Sørensen Coefficient	The **Sørensen index**, also known as **Sørensen's similarity coefficient**, is a statistic used for comparing the similarity of two samples. It was developed by the botanist Thorvald Sørensen and published in 1948.
Stop Words	Stop words are less significant words like conjunctions or prepositions that may not be meaningful to your analysis. Stop words are exempted from Text Search Queries or Word Frequency Queries.
SurveyMonkey	**SurveyMonkey** is an online survey development cloud-based company, founded in 1999 by Ryan Finley. SurveyMonkey provides free, customizable surveys, as well as a suite of paid back-end programs that include data analysis, sample selection, bias elimination, and data representation tools. In addition to providing free and paid plans for individual users, SurveyMonkey offers more large-scale enterprise options for companies interested in data analysis, brand management, and consumer-focused marketing. Since releasing its enterprise in 2013, business-focused services, SurveyMonkey has grown dramatically, opening a new headquarters in downtown Palo Alto.
Twitter	A social networking website where users post 'tweets' that contain a maximum of 140 characters.

Uncoding	The work that deletes a given coding of a document at a certain Node.
Validity	The validity of causal inferences within scientific studies, usually based on experiments.
Value	Value that a certain Attribute can have. Similar to 'Controlled Vocabulary'. Example: male, female.
Zotero	A reference handling software tool.

INDEX

A
Aggregate, 95, 205
Annotations, 91, 205
Application Preferenses
  Audio/Video tab, 34
  Display tab, 33
  General tab, 32
  Labels tab, 34
  Notifications tab, 33
  Text tab, 35
Atlas.ti, 16
Attributes, 103
audio formats, 65
Autocode, 162, 205

B
Boolean Operator, 205
Broad Context, 32, 138, 145

C
Case Node, 205
Child Node, 99
Classifications, 103
Classifying, 157
closing NVivo, 44
Cluster Analysis, 205
Codable, 157
Coding Comparison Queries, 185
Coding Context, 123
Coding Density Bar, 124, 125
Coding Panel, 117
Coding Queries, 140
Coding Stripes, 124
color marking, 24, 125
Comparison Diagrams, 199
compress project, 44
Concept Map, 206
Copy, 27
Copyright, 2
Coverage, 122, 206
creating
  a Child Node, 99
  a Document, 47
  a folder, 21
  a Hierarchy Chart, 193
  a Media Item, 68
  a Memo Link, 88
  a Memo Link and a Memo, 88
  a Mind Map, 189
  a Node, 97
  a Picture Log, 81
  a Set, 28
  an Annotation, 91
  an Attribute, 106
  an Hyperlink, 93
  subfolders, 21
current user, 183

D
Datasets, 157
deleting
  a Folder, 22
  a Hyperlink, 94
  a Memo Link, 89
  an Item, 25
  graphical items, 192
dendrogram, 206
Description, 40
Detail View, 25
dialog box
  Attribute Properties, 107
  Audio Properties, 67, 69
  Case Classification Properties, 105
  Case Properties, 108
  Coding Comparison Query, 185
  Delete Confirmation, 89
  Document Properties, 23, 46
  Export Options, 48, 76, 90, 101, 115
  External Properties, 49
  Folder Properties, 22
  Font, 54
  Import Internals, 46
  Mind Map Properties, 189

Node Properties, 97
Picture Properties, 79
Select Set, 28
Source Classification Properties, 106
Unsaved Query, 132, 135, 140, 142, 143
Video Properties, 67, 69
Discourse Analysis, 206
documents, 45
double-click, 55
Drag-and-Drop, 100, 117, 119
Dropbox, 188, 206

E

editing
  a Query, 146
  Pictures, 82
  text, 53, 57
EndNote, 147, 206
Ethnography, 206
Evernote, 206
Explore Diagrams, 197
Export Options, 48, 76, 90, 101, 115
exporting
  a Dataset, 162
  a Document, 48
  a list, 25
  a Media Item, 76
  a Memo, 90
  a PDF Item, 62
  a Picture Item, 82
  an External Item, 51
  Classification Sheets, 115
  Maps, 192
  Project Data, 43
External Items, 49

F

Facebook, 169, 207
Filter, 207
Focus Group, 207
folders, 21
Fonts, 54

Framework method, 207

G

Google Chrome, 169, 175, 178
Grounded Theory, 207

H

Help Documents, 201
hiding
  Annotations, 92
  waveform, 68
Hierarchy Charts, 193
Hushtag, 207

I

importing
  a Dataset, 157
  Classification Sheets, 111
  Datasets, 157
  documents, 45
  media files, 66
  Picture-files, 77
  projects, 43
  Transcripts, 74
In Vivo Coding, 121, 207
inserting
  an image, 55
  date and time, 55

J

Jaccard's Coefficient, 207

K

Kappa Coefficient, 208

L

LinkedIn, 169, 208
List View, 22
Literature Reviews, 147
log file, 203

M

Matrix Coding Queries, 142
MAXQDA, 16
Medline, 99, 208
Memo Link, 88
Memos, 83
Mendelay, 147

merging
  Nodes, 100
  Projects, 43
MeSH terms, 99, 208
Mind Maps, 189, 208
Mixed Methods, 209

N

Narrow Context, 32, 138, 145
Navigation View, 20
NCapture, 169
node template, 187
NVivo Help, 201
NVivo Server, 188

O

OCR, 209
OneNote, 179, 209
opening
  a cell, 144
  a Document, 47
  a Hyperlink, 93, 94
  a Linked Item, 89
  a Linked Memo, 89
  a Memo, 87
  a Node, 122
  an External Item, 50
  an External Source, 50

P

Paste, 27
PDF documents, 59
Pearson Correlation Coefficient, 209
Phenomenology, 209
phrase search, 135
Picture Log, 80, 81
picture-files, 77
Plain Text, 122, 126
Project Properties
  Audio/Video tab, 42
  General tab, 40
  Labels tab, 41
  Passwords tab, 41
  Users tab, 42
PubMed, 99, 209

Q

Qualitative Research, 210
Quantitative Research, 210

R

Read-Only, 124
RefWorks, 147, 210
Region, 80
Relevance, 210
Research Design, 210
Ribbon, 29
Root Term, 137

S

saving
  a Project, 44
  a Query, 132, 135, 141, 143, 145
  a Result, 137, 141, 143, 145
screenshots, 203
selecting text, 55
Service Pack, 204, 210
Sets, 28
Sibling Idea, 190
Skip interval, 34, 71
social media, 169
sociogram, 211
sorting
  Options, 24
Spread Coding, 32, 138, 145
Stop Words, 133, 211
subfolders, 21
support, 202
SurveyMonkey, 211
system requirements, 15
Sørensen Coefficient, 211

T

Tag Cloud, 134
Teamwork, 183
Text Search Queries, 134
Tips for Teamwork, 187
triple-click, 55
Twitter, 169, 211

U

unhiding

Annotations, 92
waveform, 68

V, W

Validity, 212
Values, 103
video formats, 65
viewing
  Coding Context, 123
  Coding Stripes, 124
  Highlighting Coding, 123
Wildcard, 135
visualizations
  Comparison Diagrams, 199
  Explore Diagrams, 197
  Hierarchy Charts, 193
  Mind Maps, 189
  Sunburst, 194
  Treemap, 194
  Word Clouds, 134
  Word Trees, 136
Word Clouds, 134
Word Frequency Queries, 132
Word Trees, 136

Y

YouTube, 175

Z

Zooming, 55
Zotero, 147, 212

Printed in Great Britain
by Amazon